I Volunteered
Canadian Vietnam Vets Remember

I Volunteered

Canadian Vietnam VETS Remember

BY TRACEY ARIAL

Cover design by Terry Gallagher/Doowah Design
Author photo by Pedro Gregorio

Published with the generous assistance of the Manitoba Arts Council and The Canada Council.

Printed and bound in Canada by Les Ateliers Graphiques Marc Veilleux

Canadian Cataloguing in Publication Data

Arial, Tracey, 1963-
      I volunteered: Canadian Vietnam vets remember

      Includes bibliographical references and index.
      ISBN 1-896239-14-5

1. Vietnamese Conflict, 1961-1975—Personal narratives, Canadian. I. Title.

DS558.6.C3A75 1996   959.704'38   C96-900661-6

For Dennis
Welcome Home

CONTENTS

INTRODUCTION

This book is the story of Canadians who served with the United States Armed Forces in Vietnam. To create it, Vietnam veterans from across Canada shared their personal memories with me. They told me why they went, what they saw, and what they're doing now. Their comments showed me how deeply Canada was divided over this war.

Canadians forget that while our government wasn't officially involved in the Vietnam War, its citizens were. Hundreds of companies supported the United States military effort with supplies for the duration of the war, providing jobs for 146,000 Canadians. Media in Canada ignored peace protests, explaining war strategy instead. Reporters barely mentioned the first international protest that took place on April 27, 1967, even though citizens in Edmonton, Montreal, New Westminster (B.C.), Ottawa and Toronto took part. Draft dodgers weren't welcome either: border guards defied policy to turn them away, landlords denied them shelter, and employers refused them jobs. Young Canadians saw the war on television and wanted to go. Since Canada didn't send troops, an estimated 50,000 chose to volunteer for the United States armed forces to get to Vietnam. They didn't know—and no one told them—that it was illegal. About 30,000 ended up in Vietnam.

These estimates come from Harry G. Summers Jr.'s *Vietnam War Almanac*, but no one knows precisely how many Canadians went. Veterans quote figures ranging from 3,000 to 80,000 individuals. The high figure was provided by Mike Ruggiero, President of the Canadian Vietnam Veterans–Toronto association (CVVT). "Every time we go to a landing zone [a Vietnam veteran reunion]," he said, "we find out that a lot of guys served with Canadians."

The lowest figure—3,000—is quoted by Vietnam Veterans in Canada (VVIC) member Richard Shand in an article for *Canadian Legion* magazine and on his World Wide Web page on the Internet. His estimate is based on a statistical analysis of VVIC member figures and the 1990 book *Unknown Warriors: Canadians in the Vietnam War*. Shand's estimate can safely be ignored, however, since his figure doesn't even include the one firm statistic quoted on page 346 of his source. According to the Statistical Analysis Branch of the Immigration and Naturalization Service of the U.S. Department of Justice, 3,244 Canadians in the United States forces became naturalized Americans between 1967 and 1975.

Unknown Warriors author Fred Gaffen quotes a figure of 12,000, which was provided to him in 1988 by the Veterans Administration Office of Public Affairs. When interviewed, Gaffen said that the real figure is probably higher than he was able to verify. Several people from the 3,000-member Canadian Vietnam Veterans Coalition, an informal group integrating all the CVVA and VVIC chapters, have publicly stated that 40,000 Canadians went to Vietnam. That's the same figure that was read into the U.S. Congressional Record by Senator Edward Kennedy on January 17, 1994. In a similar statement later that same year, Senator Bob Smith not only said that 40,000 Canadians served in the United States armed forces during the Vietnam War, he also claimed that 400 Canadians were killed in action and 4,000 were wounded. Senator Smith sat on the Senate Select Committee on POW/MIA Affairs from 1991 until 1993.

Two of my uncles volunteered and one served in Vietnam. The one who served in Vietnam doesn't discuss his experience. He tried to talk when he first came back, but no one was interested then. He talked with me once, but stopped short of disclosing anything I didn't already know. I guess he figures I'd never understand.

He used to be right. After all, I was only a year old when the United States government passed the Gulf of Tonkin Resolution which officially began the Vietnam War. By the time the war ended eleven years later, my memories were a potpourri of television images and newspaper stories. To me, the Vietnam War was one big image that included hippies tossing draft cards into trash can fires, the National Guard shooting students during a protest at Kent State University in Ohio, American soldiers unloading body bags in the middle of the night, and heroic draft dodgers portrayed by big-name actors like Alan Alda.

The images horrified me and made me believe that Canadians had somehow transcended Americans by staying neutral during the Vietnam War. Although two of my uncles volunteered for Vietnam, my hypocrisy never registered. In my mind, my uncles were just two isolated souls who made a mistake, not real Canadians. I was wrong.

The overwhelming support for the Gulf War in 1990 made me realize how quickly public opinion changes. I didn't believe that the United States should have intervened but everyone I knew disagreed, including my family. Like most of North America, they believed the newspaper stories and the television reports about the war, even when the army was their only source of information. I understood then the emotion that had attracted my uncles to war twenty years earlier. That's when the research for this book began.

The 1981 *New York Times* bestseller *Everything We Had* filled in some of the gaps about what my uncle went through. Written by thirty-three Vietnam soldiers, it begins with a one-page story by David Ross called "Welcome to the War, Boys."

> The guys were all new, their first couple of days in country [Vietnam], and they were all wondering what it was going to be like…. All of a sudden, four choppers came and they didn't even touch down. They just dumped bags. One of the bags broke open and what came out was hardly recognizable as a human being…. All the guys stopped laughing. Nobody was saying anything. And some people were shaking and some people were throwing up, and one guy got down and started to pray. I said to myself, 'Welcome to the war, boys.'

Vietnam was so intense that the veterans who lived through it felt let down when they returned. They also felt rejected or out of place. The negative reaction to Vietnam started as soon as my uncle returned to the United States. Anti-war sentiments were high. Children spat on returning soldiers and everyone else slurred them. "It was bad," he said. "I was more afraid of getting shot in the States than I was in Vietnam."

He hurried to Canada, but felt ignored by family and friends when he got here. "I tried to talk about it when I first came back, but no one wanted to hear about it," he said. "Now I just try not to think about the past." He joined the Royal Canadian Legion as the son of a veteran, not even mentioning that he himself had seen war. He was driven into utter isolation, not knowing if anyone else felt the same way. Just like every other Vietnam veteran in Canada, American or Canadian.

The only psychiatric study conducted on Vietnam veterans living in Canada suggests that the long-term isolation hurt them more than hatred hurt the Americans. This isolation finally ended in 1986, when several Canadians met in Washington for the Vietnam Veterans' Memorial dedication. That's when Canadian Vietnam veterans began healing themselves.

They banded together in local associations, at first just to meet, talk about their experiences, and share information. Those meetings are still the most important function of the associations. In addition, however, Canadian veterans help each other secure U.S. disability pensions and they try to clear service records. They even search for prisoners of war.

For many years, they fought traditionalist elements in the Royal Canadian Legion to include Vietnam veterans in Remembrance Day celebrations. It finally worked. The Legion admitted Vietnam veterans as full members on October 1, 1994.

The veterans have also built two memorials to Canadians who died in Vietnam—one in Melocheville, Quebec, and another which ended up in Windsor, Ontario, when it should have been in Ottawa. Veterans are still trying to construct a national memorial in Ottawa. The difficulty in placing those memorials and the emotional response of individuals to them once they appear proves that the Canadian psyche is still split between disgust with the Vietnam War and admiration for courageous people willing to put their lives on the line for their beliefs.

Canadian Vietnam veterans still fight for the recognition they deserve—not because Vietnam was a good war, but because many of the men who fought in it were good people. Every time they get any kind of recognition, they are discredited by protesters, politicians and, most hurtful of all, veterans from other wars who want to avoid their unpopularity.

Canada supported the Vietnam War, but rejected the veterans who fought it. The families of veterans who died had to search for peace in silence. The veterans who lived questioned their self-worth, searched in vain for answers to health concerns, and struggled to find trustworthy friends. While they healed themselves, their energies were diverted from other productive activities. Only now are many strong enough to serve fellow veterans, veterans' families and their communities.

The contributions that Vietnam veterans have made to Canada are immense, but they could do even more if we'd stop ignoring them and help. They only need respect for what they've been through, instead of condemnation.

CHAPTER ONE

The Decision

Amerⁱcan Bosch fuel injection pump. Fuel bowl complete. Governor connecting rod adjusting block. Rock shaft lever pin. Spark arrester. Toothed segment clamping screw. Track Frame Guide.

Almost anyone would have been confused looking at the small-parts list for a bulldozer, but Jacques Gendron was truly muddled. Just as the unilingual francophone realized that the list was in English, the phone rang. Gendron's supervisor answered.

"Hello. No, I'll be right over."

At that moment, Gendron realized that he had to learn English.

Gendron was still looking for a way to improve his English when he joined the U.S. Army in 1963. "At the time, all Quebec youth spoke French, but my first job, I went to the north coast, and my boss was English and all the papers were English," says Gendron. "I realized that if I wanted to succeed, I'd have to learn English."

Gendron decided to go to high school in Plattsburgh, New York, but his parents couldn't afford to help. After paying his tuition and room and board for the first two months, he ran out of money. He knew he had to change his strategy. He called his father. "Dad," he said, "I'm going to enrol in the army."

The U.S. armed forces don't usually accept someone without a basic comprehension of English, but Gendron got lucky. He met Sergeant Allan George, the army recruiter. Sergeant George sent Gendron for the written test. When Gendron failed that, the sergeant sent him to take a medical anyway. The army accepted him despite his lack of language skills.

The draft for Vietnam was already on, but Gendron didn't think about it. "I didn't know that I was going to Vietnam at that period," he says.

When he got his assignment for Vietnam, he also got thirty days' leave. The military gave him a pass for anywhere in the United States, but he didn't have permission to go home to Canada. "They figured that if I was from Canada," said Gendron, "I was going to go home and stay."

He phoned his father and asked him to meet him in Plattsburgh, New York. "I could have stayed in Montreal if I wanted," he says. "But I thought 'no, I signed a contract and I'm going to follow it through.'"

Claude Martin was living in the United States when he volunteered in 1963. He had been staying with relatives in California for three years, working as a machinist for his uncle. "Right out of school, and I was earning more than my father who'd worked forty-four years at the same job."

A good wage wasn't the only incentive for Martin to move in with his father's sister in 1960. He also wanted to learn English. His first language was sign language because his father and mother were deaf and mute. Although his grandfather taught him French every week, Martin needed to improve his language skills. By 1963, he knew he wanted to stay and volunteered to beat the draft.

Martin was posted in Hawaii when the U.S. Congress passed the Gulf of Tonkin Resolution on August 7, 1964. By passing the Resolution, Congress gave the U.S. military permission to retaliate after the North Vietnamese supposedly torpedoed two American destroyers, although the first ship was unharmed and the second was never attacked. The Gulf of Tonkin Resolution escalated official U.S. involvement in Vietnam from military adviser to aggressor. After that, Canadians who volunteered for the U.S. Army expected to go to Vietnam. They still wanted to escape their lives in Canada, but they also wanted to help win the war they saw on television every night.

Arthur Diabo, a Mohawk from the Kahnawake Reserve near Montreal, was living in Brooklyn when he enlisted in 1967. As a steelworker on the Varrazano Narrows Bridge, Diabo's father worked seven days a week and couldn't take time off, so he had relocated his whole family to New York four years earlier to be able to spend time with them.

Art Diabo had already finished high school when he decided to join the marines. The eighteen-year-old had a job building electrical equipment for the U.S. Navy, but it seemed that everyone he knew was being drafted or was voluntarily joining the military.

"You've got to remember back in 1966, '67, we were winning the war," says Diabo. "We could see what was going on on TV almost every night. We had no purpose in life to fill that gap between eighteen and twenty-one, so the marines were foremost in our mind."

It also seemed natural to him to do his duty as a marine. "We have the traditional Indian spirit of the warrior," explains Diabo. "As long as there are wars, there'll be Indian marines fighting in them." Back on the Kahnawake Reserve Diabo had known a number of Natives who had served as U.S. marines in the Korean War. He had great respect for them. "I was always impressed growing up to see these guys on Veterans Day, November 11th. If I was going to join the military, it was going to be the marines."

Art Diabo and his friend Eddy Brown decided to enlist in the U.S. Marine Corps under the Buddy Plan. Eddy and Art lived only a block and a half away from the marine recruiting office in Brooklyn and one day they just walked over to the federal building and signed up.

Eddy Brown was accepted immediately because he was born in the United States. Diabo, however, couldn't even prove that he was in the United States legally because he had no formal identification. The recruiter took him across the street to the immigration office.

The immigration office had catalogues of rules and regulations governing the rights to residence in the United States. A lawyer directed Diabo and his recruiter to a precedent case heard in 1927. The defendant had proved that North American Natives are not considered aliens and have special status when they cross the border between Canada and the United States. The case is still used when Natives come into conflict with the U.S. Immigration Department. Coincidentally, the defendant's name was Paul K. Diabo.

The Paul K. Diabo precedent settled Arthur Diabo's immigration problem, but he still had no passport and no right to work in the United States. Diabo used his birth certificate, which mentioned his father's name, and his father's identification to get a work visa and acceptance into the marines.

Robert Beattie was nineteen years old when he volunteered in 1967. His father who was in the Canadian Air Force stationed in Greenwood, near Halifax, Nova Scotia, asked him why he wanted to join the American army instead of the Canadian one. "If you're going to join the service," says Beattie, "it would be nice to join the war."

Just before Christmas, 1967, Beattie drove four hours to Bangor, Maine, a popular shopping destination for Canadians. He wanted to graduate in the spring. Originally, he wanted to join the air force, but all the recruiting centres were on one street. He decided to walk along to see what they had. He passed the navy office first, but he didn't want to join the navy. Then he passed the army office, but he ruled that out too. The marines were next in line. "There was a guy standing there and he had blue pants on with a red stripe down the side just like a Mountie in Canada," said Beattie. "So I thought, 'wow, that's nice. I've got to check this guy out.'"

The marine recruiter told Beattie all about Parris Island, South Carolina, where he would be trained. Beattie imagined a warm tropical island. He thought, "Oh, this is pretty good. I'm from Canada and it sounds nice and warm. Cripes, it's an island all to yourself. That's a great thing."

When he went back and told his father he had joined the marines, his father's face paled. "The marines," he said. "My God, they always send them into the worst places. They fight all the worst battles. Didn't you ever see any of the John Wayne movies?"

Beattie didn't believe his father. He was sure those movies were only about life in the Army, certainly not the marines. He only recognized his father's wisdom after arriving on Parris Island.

Al Clause was a little more worldly when he joined the marines a year later, in 1968. He was only twenty years old, but he had already been to Europe and he was ready to see the rest of the world. The marines looked like a good way to do it. "I'd heard that the marines were supposed to be the best and all this good stuff," he says. "So I figured, 'what the heck, I might as well try it.'"

Clause took a bus from Hamilton, Ontario, where he lived with his father, to the recruiting office in Niagara Falls, New York. The office wasn't accepting any more volunteers, but they gave him the forms to fill out anyway. After the recruiters in Niagara Falls told him their quota was full, Clause called Buffalo, New York. They were full too. Finally, he drove to the recruiting centre in Detroit and was accepted as a volunteer. "Twenty-four hours later I was standing on yellow footprints in San Diego."

Richard Malboeuf was seventeen in 1968 and bored with his life. School was a drag. There were no interesting jobs. There was nothing to do in Pierrefonds, Quebec. He and his friends spent all their time looking for adventure. A couple of times they stole cars for joyrides, once driving a car all the way to Montreal and walking back to Pierrefonds. It took all night. After several similar escapades, even the police knew who they were, although they were never caught. "There were a gang of us, a rowdy bunch, getting into regular stuff that kids get into," says Malboeuf.

When the John Wayne movie *The Green Berets* came out in 1968, Malboeuf saw an opportunity to prove himself. The Pentagon equipped John Wayne for this film, and it shows. *The Green Berets* supported United States involvement in the Vietnam War so overwhelmingly, many considered it little more than army propaganda.

But it was enough to convince Richard Malboeuf and many other young men like him. Soldiers were heroes. Watching them jump out of airplanes, cross bridges, and save lives, Richard

Malboeuf wondered if he could do it too.

"When I got kicked out of school, I decided to join the army. I wanted to be John Wayne. That's the mentality I had then."

He resolved to join the U.S. Army and go to Vietnam. Why Vietnam? "That's the only war we had." For Malboeuf, the idea wasn't far-fetched. He agreed with the fight against Communism and he wanted to test himself, prove that he was good enough to make it.

Because he was only seventeen, Malboeuf needed his parents' permission to sign up. When Malboeuf's father refused to sign the recruiting papers, Malboeuf said, "Look, I'm going. Either I go with your signature or I go without it. I'll do what you did. I'll take Ron's birth certificate and I'll join." Malboeuf knew his grandmother had refused to sign recruiting papers for her son to join the Canadian Army before turning eighteen, so Malboeuf's father used his older brother's birth certificate and went to do his military service in World War II anyway. Malboeuf knew he could do the same thing. His brother Ron had just turned nineteen. Malboeuf's father agreed to sign the papers, but only on the condition that Malboeuf go over in a support unit for training.

Once Malboeuf had his father's signature, he ignored the directive. Without telling his parents, he became an infantryman with the 101st Airborne. His parents didn't find out about it until he received a Purple Heart after being wounded.

Malboeuf had also assured his parents that he wouldn't be alone because he was enlisting under the Buddy Plan with his best friend, Mike Tierney. The Buddy Plan was supposed to guarantee that the two boys stayed together throughout their terms of service. Unfortunately, things didn't work out that way. "When we received our orders to report to Albany for induction, we realized that Mike's report date was the day before mine. When we contacted the recruiter, he told us it was a clerical error and would be corrected before we got to Fort Dix for basic training. It was never corrected and we never got assigned to the same unit."

Although the North American media had seemed pro-Vietnam when Malboeuf volunteered, they became decidedly anti-

Vietnam while he was following his basic training at Fort Dix, New Jersey, and jump school at Fort Benning, Georgia.

Malboeuf, along with millions of other viewers, was familiar with the Vietnam War from seeing it on television. In the early '60s, many respected broadcast journalists were in favour of United States involvement in Vietnam. Walter Cronkite, the popular host of the CBS *Evening News* and a well-known hawk at the time, reported from Vietnam in 1965. Viewers watched Cronkite visit Cam Ranh Bay. They went with him on a ground patrol and into the cockpit of a B-57 jet fighter, hearing how the United States would help win the war along the way. When Cronkite said "that's the way it is," his viewers believed him. Malboeuf was no exception.

The media began to sing a different tune after the Tet Offensive at the end of January, 1968. Eighty-eight thousand North Vietnamese attacked 105 cities and towns throughout South Vietnam, and the U.S. military announced hundreds of casualties every week until the end of February. In total, 81,000 people died in the Tet Offensive, including 3,895 U.S. soldiers and 14,300 civilians.

In March 1968, soldiers from the 11th Infantry Brigade raped, tortured and killed 109 unarmed men, women and children in My Lai. At first, the army believed their report that they had killed 128 enemy, and the unit received special commendation.

Walter Cronkite made a second visit to Vietnam shortly after the My Lai incident, but before it was public knowledge. Upon his return to the United States, he pronounced, "We better get out of it [Vietnam]. It will end in a stalemate."

Heavy battles continued for the rest of the year. The military assigned more and more soldiers to Vietnam, even recalling 24,000 soldiers for involuntary second tours in October 1968.

Meanwhile, Malboeuf was stationed with the 82nd Airborne in Fort Bragg, North Carolina, instead of going to Vietnam as he wished. "I kept requesting to be sent to Vietnam but because I was a Canadian it was tougher for me to go. I was told that there was a lot of pressure from Canada not to send Canadians." The Canadian government didn't want anyone to realize that Canadians were in Vietnam.

The number of U.S. troops stationed in Vietnam had reached

a peak of 500,000 in April 1969, when Malboeuf finally received his orders. Some veterans believed that the U.S. Army put Canadians in combat more readily than Americans so the media could report fewer Americans killed. Malboeuf doesn't think so. "When the body counts came in, they didn't say whether they were Canadians, Australians or whatever," he says. "It was American soldiers being killed."

Malboeuf knew some of those soldiers, but he couldn't imagine death. "No seventeen-year-old thinks he's going to get killed," he says. "You know, that was the furthest thing from my mind." He still believes that soldiers got killed because they either made a mistake or because it was their turn. He came home without any major wounds and he knew that the discipline had been good for him. He has no regrets. "I saw what happened to the kids who stayed at home," he says. "They got in bigger trouble. Guys that I grew up with died either in a car accident or in drug overdoses. So, who took the bigger risk?"

CHAPTER TWO

The Recruit

Mike Gillhooley, the son of a decorated World War II veteran, wanted to see the world. As soon as he turned eighteen in 1966, he left his home town of Ville St. Michel, Quebec, and drove south for about an hour to cross the border into Plattsburgh, New York. The American border official looked surprised when the eighteen-year-old Montreal boy told him he wanted to join the marines, but waved him on through.

The sweaty young Canadian took Exit 38 into Plattsburgh and parked downtown. Then he walked into the old post office searching for the marine recruiting office, or perhaps the navy. When he realized that both offices were empty, he started walking out.

The army recruiter at the end of the hall often skipped lunch for just such an occasion. Gillhooley didn't hear the army sergeant until he was right behind him.

"Where do you think you're going?" Sergeant George's voice boomed.

Gillhooley jumped. "I'm here to join the marines."

The wily sergeant's trap began as he asked, "What do you want to do a stupid thing like that for? What's your background?"

The boy started talking about his membership in the army cadets and the navy cadets, his marks in high school and his father's World War II experience. He was hooked.

"Ah, then. You're definitely army material," said Sergeant George as he pulled Mike Gillhooley into his office.

Special recruiting centres were set up next to large Canadian centres in Plattsburgh, New York, and Bellingham, Washington. (Recruiters also visited major Canadian cities in 1966 and 1967, but they stopped when their presence was mentioned in the Canadian House of Commons.)

These recruiters were all specially trained to deal with Canadian volunteers. They were to provide Canadian volunteers with letters of acceptability, automatically making them eligible for U.S. citizenship. The Canadian volunteers would take these letters to U.S. Immigration, who would provide them with a visa and a green card to work in the United States. They could then be recruited for active service.

Montrealers who volunteered for the United States army during the Vietnam war probably remember Sergeant Allen George. "Surly Al, the Soldier's pal" was so well liked by potential recruits, he managed to convince more of them to join the U.S. Army than his counterparts in cities two and three times larger. Awards covered his office wall.

Of course, Sergeant Allan George didn't think of Plattsburgh, New York, alone as his territory. He wouldn't have won many recruit citations had he relied solely on recruits from the northern New York state area, with a population of about 20,000 people. Luckily, Canada's largest city was only about an hour's drive away. Sergeant George just had to wait for the young Quebecers to show up. He knew that, given the chance, he could convince any Quebecer to join the army instead of the air force or the navy or the marines. He could speak to them from the heart because he too had crossed the border to join the U.S. military.

Sergeant George not only understood how his young charges felt, he also understood the military. He knew how to get around rules, when necessary. When Jacques Gendron failed his written English test, for example, Sergeant George sent him for a physical anyway. When Gendron passed the physical with flying colours, Sergeant George simply wrote "one year of college" on Gendron's application and processed it as usual.

Sergeant George also knew that headquarters never checked an applicant's actual home address. Since the military processed applications faster for United States residents than they did for Canadian ones, he would suggest suitable U.S. residences for Canadian volunteers. In Gillhooley's case, he suggested "12 Main Street, Plattsburgh, New York." Most border town recruiters did the same.

This practice was a contributing factor to the lack of accurate statistics on the number of Canadian volunteers involved in the Vietnam War. Canadians with official homes of record in the United States were assumed to be American citizens in official statistics. Since most of the Canadian Vietnam veterans provided a U.S. address, official statistics can be misleading. For example, only fifty-eight of 58,183 people who died or went missing in Vietnam have Canada as an official home of record, although double that number have already been identified beyond doubt as Canadians.

Sergeant George didn't think about such future problems when he put an American address on Gillhooley's application. He knew that U.S. Immigration would confirm Gillhooley's Canadian residence and a lot of other information too. Gillhooley had to get letters from three professionals as though he were getting a passport. He also had to pass a medical with x-rays to check for tuberculosis and go through RCMP security checks and fingerprinting.

The medical, the RCMP security check and the fingerprinting were for the benefit of the United States Armed Forces, but before the U.S. Armed Forces could accept a Canadian citizen like Gillhooley as a volunteer, he had to qualify for an alien registration card, also known as a temporary green card, from a U.S. consulate or embassy to avoid breaking Canadian law.

Although Gillhooley didn't know it at the time, according to Canadian law it was illegal for him to join the foreign army. The Canadian government had passed the "Foreign Enlistment Act" in 1937, and it was still in force in the 1960s. The Foreign Enlistment Act said:

> Any person, who being a Canadian national, whether within or without Canada voluntarily accepts or agrees to accept any commission or engagement in the armed

forces of any foreign state at war with any friendly foreign state…is guilty of an offense under this act.

Since Vietnam was considered a friendly state by Canada, the American military had to find a way to circumvent the Foreign Enlistment Act before it could accept Canadian volunteers. Luckily, the Act had a flaw: it made no mention of Canadian citizens. The U.S. military turned this to its advantage by concentrating on creating a system that would turn "Canadian nationals" into "American nationals" without jeopardizing their Canadian citizenship. Potential Canadian recruits never had to know about the law.

Once a recruit was inducted, however, he began to be pressured to take American citizenship. "Every month when I got paid," says Malboeuf, "they'd ask me to become an American." Malboeuf kept saying no, and kept his Canadian citizenship through two years of combat in Vietnam.

The United States Army system worked admirably. Canadian volunteers followed the process without breaking Canadian law. It wasn't until later that the system backfired. Canadian volunteers began using their visas and green cards to stay in the United States without reporting for military service. The U.S. armed forces had to stop providing letters of acceptability to Canadians in June 1971.

Once a volunteer received his visa, he was bused to a U.S. military base where he underwent three days of physical and psychological tests conducted by the army. Every moment was filled with medical exams, x-rays, multiple-choice tests, physical endurance tests, and discussions with psychologists.

Sergeant George made sure that Jacques Gendron, whose command of English was shaky, didn't meet the psychologist. But Gendron did have to do all the other tests, including the multiple choice. "I just guessed at a lot of the questions," he says, "because I didn't know what they meant." He also had some difficulties understanding instructions, especially during x-rays. "They were telling me how to place myself in front of that machine," he says. "I just stood there, not moving, so they took the x-ray anyway."

This battery of tests eliminated anyone with flat feet, a bad heart, mental neurosis, or other medical afflictions that might make them unsuited for crises. Candidates who passed went on to boot camp.

CHAPTER THREE

Boot Camp

Arthur Diabo went to boot camp at Parris Island late in 1967. The previous summer, 700,000 people had marched down Fifth Avenue in New York to support soldiers fighting in Vietnam. Troop strength in Vietnam had reached 535,000, many of them marines. Diabo could hardly wait to join them. He was eager to get through boot camp so that he could go on to infantry training.

Diabo arrived at Parris Island in the dark. "Once everybody was off the bus, they marched us to the barracks and stripped us of all our belongings," he said. "We had to turn in our watches, wallets, and any other personal items." Once the drill instructors had a recruit's wallet he'd take all the photos out and make derogatory comments just to see how the recruit reacted. Diabo was glad he didn't carry photographs.

The first night seemed to go on forever, Diabo says. "They wouldn't let us sleep. We had to sit on the floors which were very uncomfortable, but people constantly would doze off and there would be marine guys there yelling. It was the shock phase. These were just pre-shocks."

Once daylight came, Diabo's unit went for chow. To chow down was to refuel and it was rarely pleasant.

For the first three weeks of boot camp, platoons had to line up for every meal. Before leading his platoon to a table in the mess hall, the platoon guide asked permission to speak to the drill instructor. The drill instructor's answer might be "Speak up, worm." Then the guide had to request permission for his platoon to go to chow. When permission was granted, the platoon did not walk, but ran, to sit down. Recruits were not allowed to speak while they chowed down. They couldn't relax. The drill instructor hovered until everyone in a platoon ate every chunk of food he'd been given. Claude Martin remembered one recruit who feared his drill instructor so much, he vomited into his plate. The drill instructor made him eat it.

When Diabo got to Parris Island, the U.S. Marine Corps had just shortened basic training from twelve weeks down to eight. The drill instructors would need every moment to prepare the privates for active war duty. Boot camp is designed to either condition you both physically and mentally or break you, says Diabo. "Physically, you're in with a lot of different people, all different sizes and shapes. Some are conditioned already and others aren't. There's obviously some people who just can't take it. Psychologically, people can be broken. They get rooted out. Whatever's left are the people they'll turn into marines."

It all began with the haircut. Everyone got a skin head.

After that, the recruits had to pack all their civilian clothes. Although army recruits were allowed to store their personal belongings at the top of their lockers, marines had to pack theirs up and send them to their families at home. "They let you write a brief note," says Diabo. "They tell you what to write, basically saying that you've arrived OK and everything's OK and that they'll be hearing from you in a few weeks."

Then the drill instructors started loading recruits down with equipment to carry. First, duffel bags, uniforms, T-shirts, and boots.... "You don't know what it is," says Diabo, "but it's uniforms that you're going to be using throughout your marine career." From then on, everybody looked exactly alike, except for size and colour.

Everything happened fast. They went for pictures. They went to have their teeth checked. They went for vaccinations.

After all that was done, they went back to join their platoons to sleep. When they woke up, it was to bright lights and three drill instructors hurling garbage cans, ordering them around, and calling them names.

That's when the real training started.

Recruits had to learn to operate well in extreme heat and uncomfortable situations. "You're constantly on the go," says Diabo. "You can't talk, you can't speak to anybody. The whole environment is alien to you. It's hot. People are yelling. You're constantly running." The most important exercises conditioned recruits to get used to being wet. "If it's raining, you're going to sweat anyway," says Diabo. "You're wet when it's damp because you're in the bush. You're wet if you're going through a swamp. It's extremism. You're either too dry or too wet. There's no use complaining about it, you're going to be wet anyway. So you be happy in your wetness."

"Everything is planned for you," says Diabo. "You know what you're going to be doing at a certain time and you know how many hours that will be. You know how many minutes you're going to be marching. Routine is not broken."

"All the training works," says Diabo, who still applies his boot camp training in many situations. "I'm a neat freak. I keep my hair neat, it's always cut properly. I'm always clean-shaven. My wife complains that if I'm shovelling snow, it has to be in a straight line. It's got to be neat. You graduate a marine and you're a marine for the rest of your life."

Robert Beattie was glad to abandon the March cold in Canada, so he didn't mind the thirty-two-hour non-stop bus ride through Charleston to Parris Island. He spent the time dreaming of a tropical paradise. When the bus pulled into the Marine Corps base, Beattie caught his breath. "I thought there was some mistake," says Beattie. "I didn't go to the right island."

Beattie had imagined blue skies, wide expanses of beach, white sand and green palm trees. When he got off the bus at Parris Island, there was lots of green. Crowds of people in green uniforms marched and ran in every direction. Green people screamed at other green people.

One of them, a drill instructor, was waiting outside the door of Beattie's bus as the first recruit stepped down. He moved so close that his nose touched the recruit's nose and yelled, "Get your gear, maggot, and line up on those footprints." He repeated the sentence to every recruit coming off the bus.

As the drill instructor berated the new recruits, Beattie wondered if he could make it through the eight-week training. Everything was loud. Shots rang out incessantly from the rifle range so that the whole place sounded like a giant jackhammer. Beattie didn't know that he'd also have to survive a drill instructor who had no qualms about crossing the line between the use of healthy fear and cruelty to motivate troops.

Beattie got on the wrong side of the drill instructor when he left his wallet in his open foot-locker. His sergeant took the wallet, after verifying that it contained money and photos. He told Beattie that he'd have to do 500 push-ups in the furnace room to get it back. "So I did it," says Beattie. "It almost killed me, but I did it."

Somehow, the fact that he had volunteered for the marines made it easier for him to accept the rough treatment. "I found that as a Canadian, I wanted to be there," he says. "I could step back from it and realize that I asked to be there. Maybe I had made a mistake, but I told myself I was man enough to get through it."

Beattie realized he'd got off lucky with 500 push-ups when he saw the same sergeant kick the teeth out of a private during a rifle competition. The Kentucky marine was an expert rifleman. "He could hit a hole right in the centre of a tin can at 500 yards. In the Marine Corps, if you could shoot like that you were in," says Beattie. "But he was a real hillbilly. I mean he had two right feet and very low intelligence."

Beattie's drill instructor decided to use this Kentucky boy to enable Platoon 135 to win the next rifle competition. He wanted to see that flag flying from his platoon's staff so that he could get the top instructor honour.

His plan was common practice, although no one else got caught doing it. He would give the Kentucky marksman three sets of ammo instead of one. The guys on either side of him would shoot blanks at the targets, so that he could get them all. With ten targets to verify, the officer marking the target would never notice the cheating.

The drill instructor then made the mistake of telling the Kentucky marksman how much was riding on him. When the time came for the final test, the private was so nervous he couldn't hit his own target, let alone the other two. "The drill instructor went crazy," says Beattie. "It was bad enough having two guys who weren't very good shots, but they didn't even have any live ammo so they couldn't even do the best they could."

The drill instructor went up to the 200-yard line where the Kentucky marksman lay. As he raised his boot to kick the young private in the side of the head, the boy turned his head. The drill instructor's army boots went right into the boy's mouth.

"The drill instructor just screamed at the young fellow and told him to keep shooting," says Beattie. "Then the young fellow spit all them teeth out and blood and everything else; he laid down and continued shooting."

That would have been the end of it if the corporal caretaker of the marines hadn't seen everything. He reported the drill instructor to the officer in charge and said that he had personally witnessed Beattie's sergeant kick the Kentucky marksman. The officer stopped all firing, which was rare, to find out what had happened.

The Kentucky boy didn't want to say anything. "He knew that he had to go back to his barracks that night with that sergeant," says Beattie. "He had more fear of him than this major he didn't even know. So he said that he fell."

"I hate to argue with a private, sir," said the corporal, "but I personally saw that sergeant kick him." The major ordered the sergeant locked up.

Although Beattie hadn't told anyone about his own incident, he was asked about it during the drill instructor's hearing. He could only surmise that the incident had been reported by college-dropout officers who went through basic training as spies. "At the time, a lot of college dropouts went through as officers," he says. "Well, what do you do with 500 officers? They would put them through Parris Island and ask them to write up a report about exactly how they were treated."

In the end, both the corporal and the sergeant in charge of Platoon 135 were court-martialled and sent to Vietnam as privates. It was one of the few times a drill instructor had been court-martialled since World War II. The date was March 1968.

Meanwhile, Al Clause, a twenty-year-old Canadian from Hamilton, Ontario was starting his own pilgrimage to join the marines. After finally being accepted at the Detroit recruiting office he was sent to boot camp in San Diego. Recruits who lived east of the Mississippi went to basic training on Parris Island. Everyone else went to the San Diego Marine Corps Recruit Depot like Clause.

For Clause, the location was an advantage. From the moment he arrived, Clause felt as though he knew the base intimately. "When I got there, everything looked pretty familiar," he says, "because *Gomer Pyle* was filmed there." *Gomer Pyle, U.S.M.C.* was the third most popular television program in Canada in 1968, beaten only by *The Andy Griffith Show* and *The Lucy Show.*

On graduation day, the drill instructor decided to take advantage of Clause's constant desire for a cold beer. Clause was almost alone in this desire, because he was one of the few recruits who had already turned twenty-one. The drill instructor decided to make a punishment called "watching TV" a little more painful.

He called Clause into his office and told him to "watch TV." Clause got down on the ground to start doing push-ups, using his elbows in place of his hands. "As soon as I started shaking and quaking," says Clause, "he said that my time was almost up and I blew it."

The drill instructor told Clause to do it again, only this time he put a beer down in front of him. Clause stared. Then the drill instructor stopped him without telling him to get up. "Then he talked for a bit and I was still lying there watching that beer sweat," says Clause. "The droplets were running down. Then he said, 'Go ahead, that's yours.'"

But Clause didn't do anything because he thought it was a trick. "Well if you don't want it," said the drill instructor, "I'll drink it."

Clause grabbed the beer and sucked it back. His drill instructor let him finish it in exchange for the look on his face.

Basic training for army personnel was similar to that of the Marine Corps, although it was much shorter because there were so many more people to train. Army recruits spent six weeks at one of the twenty-four bases across the country.

Jacques Gendron took his basic training at Fort Campbell, Kentucky. "I arrived there during the night," he says. "I got off the bus and a tall coloured sergeant was yelling at us, but I couldn't speak a word of English." Gendron got through boot camp by doing exactly what other recruits in his platoon did.

Gendron couldn't watch them while he was eating, though, and that once got him in trouble during chow time. "Someone spoke and an officer told everyone to get out," he says. "But I didn't understand so I just sat there patiently eating." He only realized his mistake a few minutes later as the officer stood over him glaring.

Gendron's inability to understand English also encouraged other recruits to tease him. One night while he was sitting on his bunk, something bit him. He picked up the cot and found a dog trapped below. "I took the bed and threw it as far as I could in the barracks," says Gendron. "Everybody woke up and I asked who did it. Somebody told me it was a big guy, so I went up to him and punched him. I didn't care how big he was."

Such boot camp experiences were typical and they may have caused post-traumatic stress disorder (PTSD), a type of nervous anxiety in individuals who undergo extreme trauma. Claude Martin, a Canadian who served with the Marine Corps for six years (four years' active duty, including a tour in Vietnam, and two years' inactive reserve) believes that boot camp itself could cause the affliction. It begins, he says, with a regimented system that destroys individuals. Every morning, a company of 200 men must quickly shit, shower and shave in time for parade inspection. All the facilities are in one area. Seatless toilet bowls on one side of a room, sinks and mirrors for shaving on the other side. Shower stalls hook onto the other side of the wall behind the toilets. One recruit moves in after another. Everyone using the toilet shines his boots at the same time, while others shave, shower, brush and floss.

Martin, who spent some time training recruits for combat, explained why drill instructors got so close when giving orders to recruits. "For him," says Martin, "he's talking down your windpipe to depersonalize you."

According to Martin, depersonalization was the first step in the training process. "The first thing they do is try to neutralize the word love by referring to women as pussy, fuck or cunt," says Martin. "They don't use the word love. They degrade women. Some of the girlfriends dumped their boyfriends right in boot camp. That was lesson number one. Then you got on a base camp far away for a year or two…there's not a girlfriend who's going to wait for you. You see a lot of Dear John letters."

Drill instructors also enforced discipline twenty-four hours a day. New recruits ran everywhere during basic training. "The only time you walked was on the way to sick bay," says Martin. "Then you wouldn't walk, you'd march."

Sometimes fear motivated recruits to do things they never dreamed possible. Martin once saw a marine swim the full length of a pool because he feared his drill sergeant so much. The marine didn't know how to swim.

"Like everybody else, I hated my drill instructor at first," says Martin. "Then afterwards you respect him for what he is. That guy's a machine. The drill instructor did the same exercise that I did and then he said, 'OK everybody, down for 100 push-ups.' He pumped 100 push-ups too. I couldn't keep up with him and I was younger than he was."

Martin used to train recruits for combat situations at Camp LeJeune. "I had a lot of officers who came to see me because I had more experience than they had," he says, "because I was in Panama twice."

One drill was designed to teach a marine how to sacrifice himself for the good of his troops. It consisted of four army troops guarding fifteen to twenty marines, including Martin. Martin told the other marines to run away as soon as he jumped on the number four guard. He himself crossed a crocodile river to try to get away.

When the army recaptured Martin, they put him on a board truck with six other marine prisoners. The guards didn't know that the marines had had an additional week of training during which they learned to jump off trucks. The truck stopped and the marines jumped off.

Another drill took place in a prisoner-of-war compound. By this time, the guards knew enough to leave Martin alone in the corner to stop him from helping other marines. He still managed to slide close to a Black Beret. Martin suggested a way for the Black Beret to help relieve his buddies from a torturer who put molasses on them to attract red ants. "Call him a black bastard," said Martin, who knew that the white torturer would stop what he was doing to argue with the black man.

Martin believes that the training marines received was as good as it could be, but it can't possibly compare to experience. "The ones who were sent directly from boot camp to Vietnam," he says, "got two months' training."

CHAPTER FOUR

Tours of Duty

It took only two hours to escape the noise and dirt of the city. They drove east and south until they reached a small town at the end of a long peninsula jutting towards the Mekong River Delta. Their destination was Ving Tau beach, a locale known to the French as Cap St. Jacques. If Vietnam is a long shark with a North Vietnamese tail and a Saigon mouth, they were heading to the tooth in the shark's mouth.

As the gentle waves of the South China Sea lapped onto the sand, their music replaced the helicopter and plane noise that Jacques Gendron usually heard. He was grateful to his French friend for inviting him on the outing.

When Jacques Gendron arrived in March 1964, one year and one week after the U.S. Army Advisory Campaign began, he was one of an estimated 21,000 soldiers in Vietnam. South Vietnam was in political upheaval. Generals and marshals from various factions within the South Vietnamese Army were taking turns running the government after the assassination of Ngo Dinh Diem the previous November.

General Nguyen Khanh was running South Vietnam when Gendron arrived. Khanh had replaced a military junta led by General Duong Van Minh on January 31, 1964. The U.S. advisers subsequently learned that Communist factions in South Vietnam were being equipped by North Vietnam, China and the Soviet Union via a supply trail in Laos. Air strikes targeting that trail began in February.

U.S. soldiers like Gendron were supposedly in Vietnam to

advise and train South Vietnamese Army personnel. Gendron found himself working at a warehouse in Tan Son Nhut airport, near Saigon. By day, he recorded equipment arriving from the United States and worked on aircraft maintenance.

At night, Gendron sneaked off the base to Lily's Bar in downtown Saigon or to the home of one of several Vietnamese friends he'd made. The Québécois youth preferred the company of local Vietnamese over fellow American soldiers because he enjoyed speaking his native language. "Most Vietnamese who were thirty or over spoke French," he says. "So I got to know them quite well." His ability to converse in French led to Gendron's friendship with the Frenchman and the subsequent visit to the beach at Cap St. Jacques.

Gendron, his French friend and a Vietnamese man who had been invited to join them were basking in the sun when a young child approached them. The child said something that made the three men jump up and practically run towards the Frenchman's Citroen to drive away.

As the Frenchman and his two guests drove towards Saigon, they came upon a roadblock manned by men with rifles. Gendron didn't know who they were. "They weren't from the regular Vietnamese army," says Gendron. "They were wearing army shirts and pants like Americans."

The Frenchman stopped the Citroen, and one of men at the roadblock put the butt of his rifle against passenger Gendron's head. They said to the Frenchman, "He's American." Gendron had borrowed shorts, a shirt and sandals from his French friend for the trip, but he knew that his short haircut gave him away.

Gendron stared straight forward but he could feel the cold metal against his head. The Vietnamese man holding the rifle was speaking, but Gendron was too frightened to listen through the accent. "He just kept talking slowly in French to the French guy, but I don't really know what happened," says Gendron. "Eventually the Vietnamese guy in the seat behind me started talking to the other guy in Vietnamese and the French guy slowly inched the car forward. This guy still had the rifle to my head and he kept saying 'American, American, American.'"

Finally, the Vietnamese fellow in the back seat of the Citroen pushed aside the end of the other man's rifle. Gendron still doesn't know who the Vietnamese at the roadblock were, but he now knows the identity of the Vietnamese man he travelled with. "The French guy told me later that this Vietnamese guy was Viet Cong. One of his sons was in jail."

Viet Cong (Vietnamese Communist) was the nickname Diem gave to a coalition group which had formed on December 21, 1960. The group's actual name was the National Liberation Front (NLF). At first, NLF contained both Communist and anti-Communist interest groups whose common goal was to overthrow the Diem government and institute social reform and political independence for South Vietnam. Hanoi began publicly supporting the NLF and their guerrilla tactics in South Vietnam in January 1961.

Later that summer, President Kennedy announced that "the United States is determined to help Vietnam preserve its independence, protect its people against communist assassins, and build a better life through economic growth." That led to the creation of the U.S. Military Assistance Command Vietnam (MACV) in February 1962. The first U.S. Army regular unit—39th Signal Battalion—arrived in Vietnam a month later.

Several events in 1963 led to a wider infiltration of the Viet Cong as well as Diem's disfavour with the U.S. government and his eventual ousting and assassination. Members of the Buddhist majority in Vietnam joined Viet Cong ranks after peaceful protests not only failed to end religious discrimination by the Catholic Diem administration, but ended in violence against the protesters. The first incident occurred in Hué on May 8, 1963, when the South Vietnamese Army fired into a crowd during a Buddhist celebration.

Within a week, a Buddhist monk named Thich Quang Duc brought the issue to Saigon by burning himself to death. Sympathizers rioted throughout Saigon until Diem's troops fired on them. After a second monk committed self-immolation in August, police raided Xa Loi, a major Buddhist pagoda, and Diem extended martial law throughout South Vietnam. The resulting student demonstration on August 25 led to several arrests. While Buddhist monks continued to use self-immolation to protest against their government over the next two years, other

TOURS OF DUTY / 39

Buddhists and many students joined the Viet Cong guerrilla campaign instead.

By the time Gendron got there in 1964, there was heavy Viet Cong infiltration in the South Vietnamese Army. "If you were working with ten people," says Gendron, "three or four were Viet Cong."

The effect the Viet Cong infiltrators had on U.S. military goals upset Gendron. "I was in Supply so I knew that Vietnamese were loading Vietnamese bombers that would drop the bombs into the ocean and come back and say they destroyed such and such a place," he says. "Later, they put one American and one Vietnamese together to fix that, but the Vietnamese did it a long time before they got caught."

Gendron also became depressed with the constant killing of American soldiers like himself. "I remember the coffins we received," he says. "We had maybe twenty or thirty in a week and every day they were taking some until they were gone. We sent the dead bodies back to the States."

By the time Gendron left Vietnam, in March 1965, 246 American GIs had been killed and another 1,641 were wounded. The U.S. Advisory Campaign officially ended on March 7, 1965, five days after the U.S. began bombing North Vietnam.

By then, Blair Seaborn, Canada's International Control Commissioner in Vietnam, had personally delivered four out of five messages from the U.S. president to North Vietnamese prime minister Pham Van Dong in Hanoi.

Seaborn led a staff of almost 100 Canadians who were supposed to oversee the truce between North and South Vietnam that had been set out in the 1954 Geneva Conference on Indochina. Canada and Poland served under India's leadership.

Seaborn's early visits to Hanoi warned the North Vietnamese about the possibility of bombing by the United States, while the last two were attempts to negotiate a settlement after bombing in the North had already started. The North Vietnamese response can be summed up by Dong's words to Seaborn at his second visit on August 13, 1964, when he said, "We do not hide the fact that the people will have to make many sacrifices, but we are in a state of legitimate defence because the war is imposed upon us."

Dong's words reflected the North Vietnamese assertion that the war in South Vietnam was an internal one between the NLF (Viet Cong) and the military factions controlling the South Vietnamese government. The United States did not agree with that assertion, however, and neither did Canada.

Seaborn stated Canada's position in a minority report submitted by the International Control Commission to the Geneva co-chairmen. Britain released Canada's report with the majority report signed by India and Poland on March 8, 1965.

India and Poland wanted the Geneva co-chairs to officially ask the United States and North Vietnam to stop the escalation of the war and achieve peace. Canada's report blamed the North Vietnamese government for all attempts to overthrow the government in South Vietnam and the resulting bombing by the U.S. military. Seaborn included a list of captured weapons which had originated in communist countries (China, Czechoslovakia, East Germany and the U.S.S.R.). The report helped justify bombing that had already started on March 2.

While the international community and the U.S. military concentrated on bombing North Vietnam, an operation they called "Rolling Thunder," the marines arrived in Vietnam with a different goal. Claude Martin, another Canadian from Quebec, arrived with them.

Martin's tour of duty in Vietnam began in March 1965 with "K" Company, 3rd Battalion, 4th Marines. They had been training in Okinawa when orders came in to board the U.S.S. *Enrico.* It began to get very hot. "As the temperature rose," says Martin, "it was the middle of night and they said, 'See those lights over there? That's Vietnam so that's where you're landing tomorrow.'"

Martin and his group weren't sure if they were practising or if the landing really would occur until they checked the gas tanks. "The gas tanks were full, the water tanks were full and they started to pass live ammo," says Martin. "So we knew we were facing the real McCoy."

The 4th Marines landed on an island south of Da Nang the next morning. The 1st and 2nd Battalions wen to Chu Lai, while Martin joined the 3rd Battalion in Phu Bai, a small town just north of Da Nang and about fifteen kilometres south of Hué. Martin's group set up security around the Phu Bai airport.

Martin spent the next few months with the infantry. Infantrymen were the ones who walked through, or flew over, the jungle trying to get the North Vietnamese to attack them. Their only job was to shoot, blow up, or use their bayonets to stab the enemy—whom they called Charlie—until he died. If they couldn't kill Charlie themselves, they called in artillery and air strikes.

Martin didn't mind infantry, but his favourite job began in 1966 when he was assigned to the Combined Action Platoons, also known as the Combined Action Company, and the Combined Action Program (CAP) Marines.

CAP was a pacification program designed to discourage Vietnamese from working with the Viet Cong. It placed the best marines, those who won competitions at Camp Pendleton, into Vietnamese villages to live. The unit based in Phu Bai 3 had one open position for Martin. "I was not specially trained," says Martin. "These guys were good, but I joined them because I spoke French and the chief of the village spoke French." Martin interrogated suspicious Vietnamese villagers with a French police officer from Hué and an officer from S2, the U.S. military intelligence force.

CAP marines did whatever was necessary to improve their communities. In total, their "Operation Golden Fleece" program built 1,253 schools, 175 hospitals, 153 public markets, 263 churches, 223 pharmacies and medical centres, 598 bridges, 7,100 houses and 3,153 kilometres of roads. They taught 212,000 villagers how to take care of their skin, teeth and hair. They also provided 600,000 pieces of soap, by soliciting partially used bars left behind in American hotels.

Despite their successful peace efforts, CAP marines like Martin had to join all the other infantry units' patrols throughout their area in looking for Viet Cong. It was difficult, though, because many families were split—half were pro-government, the other half Viet Cong.

If marines found someone they assumed to be Viet Cong, they had to capture or kill him. Excellent observation skills were needed to determine whether Viet Cong were in the neighbourhood or not. Martin remembers seeing a hutch near a river with a chicken in it laying eggs. The first day they checked for eggs and found them. So the next day, they checked again. When the eggs were still there, Martin's squad knew that the hutch was Viet Cong. Other villagers were poor and would have needed those eggs. "So we set up an ambush," says Martin.

Martin saw a lot of atrocities committed by the Viet Cong. Villagers who cooperated with the Americans were often killed or maimed. Martin particularly remembers one seventeen-year-old girl who refused to help the Viet Cong set a trap for the Americans. The Viet Cong chopped her right foot off.

Viet Cong patrols also tried to kill marines. One day, while on patrol, Martin and Ron Casto, a fellow marine, heard the Vietnamese using their own Mutter 3 radio code to call headquarters. The two marines were located between headquarters and the source of the false call, and Mutter 3 was their code. Martin realized then just how good the Viet Cong were. Casto quickly got on the radio to inform headquarters about the false call. "Six, this is three," he said. "Ignore the ede bone signals."

The Viet Cong tunnel system was particularly ingenious. Some were built on two levels, so that marines would be walking above Viet Cong hiding below. CAP marine patrols searched for tunnels in the villages, but they had to be careful. Villagers built their own civilian tunnels to protect themselves from artillery. The Viet Cong tunnels were usually harder to find. The marines often found them in pigpens, because the Viet Cong thought Americans wouldn't go through the manure.

Most of the time, people in a civilian tunnel would respond to marine calls, but sometimes they were too frightened. If they had tear gas grenades, the marines used them to clear a tunnel, but they often had none. Martin remembers a fellow marine who once used a regular hand grenade instead, and killed about fifteen kids. After that, Martin went into suspicious-looking tunnels himself with a flashlight and a .45-calibre pistol.

"Tunnels had scorpions and centipedes and you had to squash them as you went along," says Martin. "There was also a viper that we called Mr Two-Steps. If you got bit, you would probably die, even if you got medical attention. All you could do was light up a cigarette and see whether you or it would die first."

Most of the CAP marines that Martin worked with were

killed in action. T.O. Green, one of the first to be killed, died in Martin's arms after a bullet he'd taken in the shoulder ricocheted down to his heart. Martin's own close call with death came a short time later. "A North Vietnamese trooper was no farther than ten feet from me and he had me," he says. "He fired his automatic weapon but the round didn't go off, because they had bad ammunition." In the end, only he and Casto survived their full thirteen-month Vietnam tours. Martin was glad to leave Vietnam in April 1966. He got back to North America in time to see the Montreal Canadiens take the Stanley Cup for the second time in a row.

Eight months later, both North and South Vietnam agreed to their first forty-eight-hour truce at Christmas 1966. Cease-fires also occurred during the American New Year and the Vietnamese New Year (Tet) from February 8 to 12, 1967.

But on February 14, the United States began bombing North Vietnam again. Protests against the Vietnam War began two months later when 100,000 people demonstrated in New York and San Francisco. In May, the United States and South Vietnam moved into the Demilitarized Zone for the first time and the United States bombed a power plant within a mile of Hanoi.

Meanwhile, Mike Gillhooley was waiting in Alabama hoping to go to Vietnam. "Apparently, they were confused about what to do with a Canadian," he says. "They didn't know whether to send me to Vietnam or to send me to Germany or what to do with me. I taught martial arts at the training centre until my orders for Vietnam came in."

He had already been stationed at Fort McClellan for six months when his orders finally arrived in the fall of 1967. His commanding officer called him into the office. "Specialist, I got your orders for Vietnam, but you have a choice," he said. "You're Canadian, so you can go home and not come back. I would highly recommend that for you." Gillhooley took the one-month leave he was entitled to, but he knew he'd be back.

When Gillhooley told his Canadian friends he was going to Vietnam, their response was "OK, have a good time."

He thought about them as he was getting off the plane at Tan Son Nhut airport, near Saigon. "I couldn't breathe because of the heat," he says. "I had gone through seventeen days hard jungle training in heat but it was nothing like Vietnam. I just couldn't breathe. And the smell. The whole place smelled different. I had never encountered a smell like that before." Have a good time? His friends in Canada had no idea.

He thought about his friends again as he was landing in An Khe. The transport plane pilot had turned the engine off to glide in. Then the pilot came onto the intercom with instructions. "I'm going to open up the tailgate and I'm going to coast down the runway," he said. "You guys are going to have to run out the back because we're under rocket attack."

The new soldiers looked at one another in shock. They didn't have weapons, flak jackets, helmets or anything else yet, and they had no idea where they were supposed to go. The air force crew on the plane didn't know the army base well enough to give them directions. As the plane slowed down, the soldiers unstrapped themselves, grabbed their gear, and prepared to run out.

The back door folded down and soldiers poured out, some running left and others right. "I went left and I was lucky," said Gillhooley. "I wound up in a bunker. Some guys went right and they were right in the middle of the airstrip. So they had to turn around and come back the way I was."

All at once, Gillhooley saw the sandbags. Rockets were coming in, leaving a trail of fire as they landed. The soldiers already in the bunkers started yelling at him, "Get out. What are you doing in here?" as if he should have known better.

"Hey man," said Gillhooley. "I just got out of this plane, what are you telling me?" That's when they started calling him names.

"Ah, Turtle, get in the corner because you don't know anything. Fucking new guy."

During his term with the 1st Air Cavalry in the Central Highlands of South Vietnam, Gillhooley survived firefights from the air as a gunner, and from the ground as a mortarman. The mortarman position was worse. The enemy knew to concentrate their rockets on the mortar pits, so he was always in danger. To make matters even worse, he could never see what was going on. "I wouldn't know who I was aiming at. They'd call in and say, 'We need mortar rounds at such and such a position.' I didn't

want to know what I hit, but it would be nice to see the target."
Several times Gillhooley had to try to hit Viet Cong within 200
metres of American infantry. Sometimes, the enemy got so close
Gillhooley had to kill them with his rifle or pistol.

When Gillhooley was working as a gunner he became
famous, thanks to a *Stars and Stripes* article written about a stunt
he pulled three months into his tour. Gillhooley waved the
Canadian flag as he hung out the side of a helicopter. When the
pilot asked what the hell he was doing, Gillhooley said, "I'm
trying to confuse Charlie. I don't think he's seen this flag before."

The pilot didn't laugh. "Well, you put it inside," he said, "or
you're going to be Article Fifteened [military discipline action]."

Gillhooley was supposed to leave in the fall of 1968. He had
been counting down the days but then he received a letter from
his brother, who had signed up for the U.S. military a year after
Gillhooley. He was based in Korea when he wrote to say he'd
received orders for Vietnam. Gillhooley flipped. He didn't want
his brother anywhere near Vietnam.

Luckily, Gillhooley had heard of the law—the Sullivan
Clause—which obligated the army to keep at least one surviving son in a safe zone. Congress had passed the Sullivan Clause
during World War II, after five brothers were killed, leaving no
one to carry on the family name. The navy had posted the
Sullivan brothers together on the same ship which went down
in the bombing of Pearl Harbor.

Gillhooley's commanding officer told him that he could prevent his brother from serving in Vietnam only by extending another tour. Gillhooley agreed on the condition that he be assigned
a different specialty. He was tired of blowing people up.

Gillhooley's plan worked. His brother went off to Germany
and Gillhooley was reassigned to the 507 Transportation group
in Saigon, primarily because he could speak French. "I thought
it was going to be a piece of cake because I was in Saigon," he
says. It didn't turn out that way.

The 507 Transportation group was responsible for security
in the Cholon (Chinatown) district of Saigon. Viet Cong armies
had concentrated on the Cholon district when they attacked Saigon from May 25 until June 4, 1968, and they still maintained a
heavy presence there when Gillhooley arrived.

Gillhooley was responsible for getting information from the Cholon-area orphanages because the nuns who ran them were French. "I had to get their confidence because they didn't just trust anyone," he says. "So I would do silly things like bring loads of blankets for the orphanages, or bring them in food."

Gillhooley knew that the Viet Cong stole the orphanage food and blankets at night, so he constantly replaced them. His goal was to find out exactly what time the Viet Cong came in and via which roads or canals. It never worked. The nuns called Gillhooley "Capitaine Michel" and he had their trust, but it didn't get him anywhere.

Gillhooley's not sure he would have reported anything they told him anyway. "If I could get away with not telling," says Gillhooley, "which in some cases I probably did, I didn't tell because I didn't feel comfortable about it. You've still got a conscience you have to deal with."

"The whole project was a failure," says Gillhooley, "but the thing is, that orphanage never did get attacked. I felt good about that because they never touched the orphanage when they came through Cholon to attack the major U.S. bases."

When Art Diabo arrived in Da Nang on January 10, 1968, the Tet Offensive, the war's largest offensive, was about to begin. When a scheduled truce for the Vietnamese New Year (Tet) was cancelled, the Viet Cong and North Vietnamese responded with fury. They attacked 105 cities throughout South Vietnam, killing 14,300 civilians and almost 4,000 American soldiers. A total of 81,000 people died between January 31 and February 26, 1968.

Airstrips were under constant attack. "We had no idea what was going on," says Diabo. "It was [necessary to] run off the plane into the bunkers, because the plane couldn't sit on the airstrip too long."

All the people yelling and screaming at him to tell him where to run reminded Diabo of boot camp. He stared at all the guys getting ready to leave. After thirteen months, they looked more like jungle animals than marines. "I saw every style of mustache and unauthorized uniform," he says. "People yelled and cursed at me for no other reason than I was clean and they weren't."

Diabo didn't realize that he'd look worse than they did by the time he left.

Diabo found out that he was in trouble when he arrived at his unit. The 3rd Battalion, 5th Marines were based southwest of Da Nang. "They had just gotten hit the week before and there were just a handful of men left," says Diabo. "When I got into the staging area, we were just hearing stories about what had happened before. These guys were scared. We were finally going to see action, but they were telling us not to look forward to it, because we might not last a month. They never saw so much action in their whole tour of Vietnam as they had in the prior two weeks."

Diabo made it through his first month, but in May he was wounded by a rocket-propelled grenade. His wound wasn't serious enough to send him home, but it did get him a ten-day hospital stay in Cam Ranh Bay. Diabo should have stayed longer, but he was anxious to return to his unit. "I felt that I had abandoned my squad at a bad time," he says. "I felt that they needed me and I should get back to them as fast as I could."

Forty-eight hours after leaving the hospital, he was back in An Hoa and in the bush. Two weeks later, he walked into an ambush. "It was on an area known as the Arizona Territory, just a little bit northwest of An Hoa combat base, about fifty miles south-west of Da Nang," says Diabo. "That particular area of Vietnam was probably the most concentrated booby-trapped area in-country. You couldn't walk, sit or sleep without standing on a booby trap. There were always people tripping them and blowing up."

Diabo's unit knew that the North Vietnamese Army (NVA) concealed themselves behind every tree-line. Marine procedure was to trip the ambush and then call in air strikes, so that's what they did. When the ambush began, bullets flew from every direction. Diabo saw three people ahead of him killed and knew he had to do something. He and the rest of the line behind him jumped off the dike into a rice paddy.

From his trapped position between the U.S. Marine Corps to the rear and the North Vietnamese in front, Diabo heard the NVA sergeant barking commands at his men. Diabo knew that the

Vietnamese would concentrate their fire on him. "I had one decision to make," he says. "You've got to remember that I had a fifty-pound pack on my back, and a five-pound helmet on my head. I could either lie in that paddy and die in a few seconds or try to jump the dike that I had just hurled myself off." Diabo flipped his pack and threw his helmet off and ran. He just tried to stay clear of the green (Vietnamese) and red (American) tracers that signified rounds all around him. He dived over a paddy dike just as a bullet flipped him into a somersault. He landed in the paddy behind the dike, safe from the North Vietnamese.

Diabo's unit stopped firing when they saw what he was doing, but Diabo knew the NVA would use the lull to move forward. With all his strength, he got up and ran toward the second paddy dike. He managed to flip over the dike, but he landed in a patch of thorny bamboo, a common Vietnamese prickly vine that resembles barbed wire. A couple of the marines from his unit rescued him from there. "I could feel these guys pulling at my feet, just yanking me through the bamboo," he says. "It cut me up."

Diabo didn't notice how badly his arm was injured until he reached relative safety. Multiple fractures left half of it dangling by the flesh. Bone jutted out midway through his forearm. Diabo let the corpsmen put it into a natural position, and began conditioning himself to lose it. He knew that his "million dollar" wound would get him home. He'd be home in time for the summer of 1968.

The medivac took Diabo and another marine who had also escaped the rice paddy to Charlie company, 1st Medical Battalion, in Da Nang. Diabo heard the medical staff demanding to have his face cleaned so that they could see what he looked like. Then they began cutting his uniform off from the boots to the collar. As it dropped to the floor, two hand grenades fell out. Diabo had taped them, so he knew they weren't going to go off, but the senior corpsman didn't. "Why wasn't he checked on the way in?" he yelled.

Canadian Robert Beattie had it easier with his tour, which began in September 1968. He was boat master of a C-130 cargo plane, stationed with a Marine Corps air squadron out of Da Nang.

His job was to fly people and equipment all over Vietnam. "All I had to do was close the back door," he says. "Once all the cargo was in, I had to make sure it was strapped in secure in the airplane and close the door. There wasn't that much danger unless you got hit by a SAM rocket or something."

Beattie's life seemed charmed. He turned twenty-one in Vietnam on June 4. He and several friends celebrated at the military club in Da Nang. The club gave them all the free champagne they could drink.

Beattie also saw Ann-Margret perform at the 1968 Bob Hope Christmas show in Da Nang. "I was sitting so far back that I don't know whether Ann-Margret was clothed or unclothed," he says. "At least I can say I was there."

Beattie's life wasn't without danger, however. The Vietnamese would sneak in from the jungle grass to mortar the C-130 airplanes while they were landing and taking off. Beattie's barracks was also hit by mortar rounds several times. "The building pieces would fly everywhere and you were lucky that you weren't killed in it," he says. "Guys were killed—when it blows up, nothing's left."

He risked his life every time he and twelve other men patrolled the jungle around the runways. "We'd have an M-16 and we were walking through the jungle and I really didn't know what I was doing," he says. "I'd look around and see the other guys—Tom the pilot and Billy the truck driver—and I'd think that not one of us thirteen guys did this for a living. What in the hell were we doing?"

Beattie was lucky to the end; even his tour in Vietnam was cut short. Although the normal Marine Corps tour of duty in Vietnam was thirteen months, Beattie's tour in Vietnam lasted one year and four days. "President Nixon changed it so that marines only stayed in Vietnam one year because that was what everybody else did," he says. "So they called me and told me to get my stuff together to go home on the next plane."

By the time Beattie left in September 1969, Richard Malboeuf was a point man on patrol in the foothills near the Demilitarized Zone. He had learned plenty since his first day in the bush in April. The first time his unit got attacked, Malboeuf grabbed his weapon and started running towards the front as he had been trained to do. One of the more experienced guys, Pittman, saw what he was doing and threw Malboeuf onto the ground. "Where are you going?" he screamed.

"To the front. That's what we're supposed to do."

"You don't do anything unless I tell you to," said Pittman. "If you want to make it through your year, you do as I tell you, when I tell you."

From then on Pittman showed Malboeuf all the tricks he would need to survive. He taught him when to move forward and how to do it quietly. He showed him how to bivouac and how to set the claymore mines which they relied on for protection at night. He taught him how to crouch, how to watch for signs of the enemy, and how to tape his equipment so it wouldn't rattle. "The training was not as great as it should have been. It's what you learned once you got there," Malboeuf says. "That's why the majority of people who got hurt or killed did it in the first couple of months."

Malboeuf made it through his first few months, although the odds were against him. On May 13, 1969, only a month after he arrived, Malboeuf's firebase was attacked by the enemy. "The second day of setting up the base camp, we were overrun there and basically wiped out," he says. "We were something like a hundred and seventy guys on the hill. The next day we were down to about forty-five."

Instead of staying in his relatively safe bunker, Malboeuf took over one of the bunkers within enemy fire. After killing an NVA soldier who broke through, Malboeuf ran ammunition to another harder-hit bunker line. His efforts earned him a Bronze Star Medal with "V" Device for heroism in ground combat. "We were on a firebase airborne that was setting up artillery support for the assault on Hamburger Hill," says Malboeuf. "The other guys were either killed or wounded. The rest of our company (Company A, 2nd Battalion [Airborne], 501st Infantry), the guys who were left, were moved to reinforce one of the units taking Hamburger Hill."

Over a ten-day period the 3rd Brigade, 101st Airborne made eleven attempts to capture Ap Bia Mountain (also called Hill 937) against heavy artillery. The name Hamburger Hill was coined by infantry who passed 372 wounded and seventy dead soldiers lying on the hill when the whole thing ended on May 20.

Over the next few months, Malboeuf learned how hard infantry could be. "We worked out in the bush," says Malboeuf. "You'd wear the same clothes and everything for thirty-five or forty days. That's why you'd get ringworm and jungle rot. The sores all over your body would break open and get all pussy and they wouldn't go away, especially in the monsoon season, when you were wet all the time."

To survive, they needed a sense of humour about their job, says Malboeuf. The motto for his unit, "A" Troop 2/17 Air Cavalry, was "Killing is our business and business has been good." The soldiers would repeat it like a mantra when they got scared.

After spending ten months trying to draw enemy fire on the ground, Malboeuf became an aeroscout on an OH6 Loach helicopter in February 1970. The Loach would act as decoy, flying below a couple of Cobra gunships. "Because of where we worked along Northern I Corps, we couldn't really see the enemy because the jungle was so thick," Malboeuf says. "We would fly around and try to draw their fire so that the Cobras would see the multiple flashes."

As a gunner, Malboeuf was supposed to protect his helicopter while making it easier for the Cobras above. "I was beside the pilot," he says. "My job would be to return the fire, to use cover fire to get out and to use smoke grenades to mark the positions where the fire was coming from."

Their goal was to destroy the enemy using whatever means were necessary. "If it was a heavy concentration of troops, then we could call in fighter bombers," says Malboeuf. "And if it was really big, a base camp or something, then we could call in a B-52 strike that would hit usually the next day."

"Once we'd fired upon the North Vietnamese and they'd fired upon us, they'd know they'd been spotted," says Malboeuf. "By the time the B-52 strikes came in the next day, the enemy were gone. So we'd go in and do a BDA (bomb demolition assessment) the next day and we'd fake body counts." Effectiveness in Vietnam was measured in dead enemy bodies.

Al Clause arrived in Vietnam for his first tour of duty with the Marine Corps in 1969, serving as an engineer. "Engineering could have meant just about anything," says Clause, "but in my case it meant being a heavy equipment operator for cranes, bulldozers, graders and fork lifts."

In his two tours between the fall of 1969 and Christmas 1970, Clause saw four of his friends killed and he himself came close to dying twice.

In his first tour, Clause travelled throughout the Quang Tri area (Dong Ha, Cam Lo) with the 3rd Shore Battalion, unloading helicopters, airplanes, ships, trucks and convoys. On one job, he had to travel up and down the river with his equipment. "I got shot at quite regularly with sniper fire," he says.

When the 3rd Marine Division left Vietnam for Camp Courtney, Okinawa, in November 1969, Clause was in charge of a team loading ships. "We worked around the clock until we got the job done," he says. "We were loading ships for two and a half days; then the next ship didn't come in for four days or three days, so you had that rest in between. You'd pull guard duty, or you'd be cleaning the compound."

Early the next year, Clause was sent to Korea on a battalion landing team. But he found it too cold and decided to do a second tour in Vietnam. "So they sent me to Dong Ha the second time," he says. "I helped the 7th Engineers pack up and move back to the States."

Clause then joined the 1st Combat Engineers in Da Nang, just beside Marble Mountain. "From there, they sent me to Landing Zone (LZ) Baldy and my main job for a while was doing roadwork with a grader and doing the base itself," he says. "I'd have to write up reports on the road and what kind of equipment I needed to make improvements on the road. If there was a bridge or culvert that needed to be built, I'd have to make a report saying that we needed certain stuff for this area."

Once, while he was doing roadwork, a sniper bullet flew past Clause. "I put the vehicle in neutral and found a spot to take cover, hoping that one of the fellows in one of the towers was looking at me." Luckily, the sniper fire stopped.

After his job at LZ Baldy was finished, Clause trained in explosives, learning to blow up booby traps. He was stationed at

LZ Ross and was responsible for sweeping the roads every morning. "I'd be up at 3:30 or 4:00 a.m., get something to eat and then meet a sweep team at the front gate with my explosives and we'd go up the road," says Clause. "The infantry guys would provide security, the guys with the detectors would be out front looking for mines or booby traps and then we also had a Vietnamese interpreter with us and the officer and staff NCO [noncommissioned officer]. It was my duty to go out and blow the mines or the booby traps in place." In two or three months, he had only two villages to sweep and no one got hurt.

Richard Legault arrived in Vietnam in August 1970 while Clause was still destroying booby traps. From day one, everybody who spoke to Richard Legault wanted to know where he was from. Even near the end, when his French-Canadian accent was less pronounced than it had been, people still recognized it as something different. It didn't usually cause problems except with one Staff Sergeant in Qui Nhon. That staff sergeant hated Legault and all other Canadians. "He didn't like our Prime Minister Trudeau because he went to Russia," says Legault. "He made me miserable to the point where I was ready to do anything to get rid of him."

Legault had been keen to sign up for the U.S. Army in 1968. It seemed like the natural order of things. His father was American and had served in the U.S. Air Force during World War II. Besides, he was a single young man and it looked like a great adventure. "I still remember when Jean-Claude Hamel and I went across the border to a hotel in Richford, Vermont," he says. "We made friends with a few Americans there and we were celebrating with them. One of the Americans started crying because he had been drafted. Then me and Jean-Claude Hamel decided to volunteer with them, under the Buddy Plan so we could be together in basic training."

Legault wanted to go to Vietnam but he was posted to Germany. He was frustrated. "I was only twenty years old and I wanted to be on the adventure side," he says. No one wanted to go to Germany because the military was so strict. "You had to wear white gloves and shiny shoes," he says. "You were representing a country—it was like basic training every day."

Legault was ecstatic when he finally got orders for Vietnam in May 1970. Not only did he get his wish, he also got a month's leave with his fiancée Nicole in Montreal.

In the beginning, Nicole had only been a classmate's kid sister who offered to write to him. Their letters started out cordial but distant. After a while, they began telling each other intimate details about themselves. As they got to know each other, they wanted to spend more time together. During Legault's leave in the spring of 1970 they became engaged.

Legault still wanted to go to Vietnam, but it no longer seemed so important. Circumstances had changed and he had lost his enthusiasm for war. He just wanted to get married and begin family life with Nicole.

From the moment he stepped off the plane in Cam Ranh Bay, Legault couldn't wait to leave Vietnam. "The place stank like hell," he says. "That smell was particular, the smell of food, of decay; even the Vietnamese civil workers had their own way of making food and the smell was not all that good."

A mortar shell hit the base on Legault's first night. The siren went off and everyone around him ran for cover, but Legault wasn't fast enough. The corrugated metal tunnels that sheltered everyone filled quickly and no one would let him in. "Oh shit, what have I done?" thought Legault. "How did I end up in this place?"

Legault got through his tour by corresponding with Nicole. He sent her his pillowcase so that she could smell him while she slept. He sent a letter or a tape to her every day from August 1970 until August 1971.

Legault's letters reflected the changing war. It was more than a year after U.S. President Nixon had ordered a "Vietnamization" of the war and two months after the U.S. Senate had repealed the Gulf of Tonkin Resolution. Legault could see the transfer of power. "While I was there, it was common to see Vietnamese with new uniforms, new M-16s, new tanks, everything new," he says. "We 'Americans' had all the time in the world to get a second pair of fatigues. They were getting prepared to hand over the command to their own people. Americans were pulling out and the process was already started."

By the end of his tour, mortar attacks on American bases had dwindled to once a week and only one or two mortars at a time. The soldiers began to take safety for granted. One night at Qui Nhon, Legault and his buddy, Jerry Brasil from Sacramento, were watching a movie on the outdoor screen. When the sirens went off to indicate a mortar attack, Brasil and Legault decided to just sit and watch all the lifers. "There were two shots, but they weren't close," says Legault. "We saw all the people running around and all of a sudden we were all by ourselves. We defied it. The shots didn't come close, not even close enough to get the earth trembling. Then the siren went on again and everyone else came out of hiding."

CHAPTER FIVE

Welcome Home

When Claude Martin came home in 1965 he had a tapeworm that he'd picked up eating raw fish in Vietnam. "At first, I thought I had an ulcer," he says. "But I didn't have an ulcer. It was the fish tapeworm. It had suction cups and hooks and it followed my digestive tube like an onion ring."

It took eight years before Martin's doctors successfully treated the parasite. "It was puncturing a hole in my stomach," he says. "Every time I took something to kill it, it would break away, but either the head would grow a tail or it would lay eggs, and I was stuck with the problem again." Even after he finally got rid of it, Martin had to be tested every three months for five years to see if the tapeworm had laid any new eggs.

Then the growths, which look like giant pimples but are hard as rock, started popping up on the back of his head. Usually, Martin has them removed, but sometimes they fall off by themselves. He also suffers from unexplained sneezing attacks which can go on for fifteen minutes or more.

Martin blames these health problems on Agent Orange, which he originally knew as Agent Purple, because of the colour of the liquid. Agent Orange was heavily sprayed in the Phu Bai area, especially near the marine base where Martin served.

Agent Orange was a very effective defoliant, and the U.S. Army used the herbicide throughout Vietnam. At the time, the chemical companies manufacturing it assured the U.S. military that the substance was harmless to humans. Since then, studies have shown that Dioxin, the main ingredient in Agent Orange, is a proven carcinogenic.

In 1980, Vietnam veterans received a $180 million settlement from a class action suit against seven of the chemical companies responsible for the manufacture of Agent Orange, including Dow Chemical, Uniroyal, Monsanto, Hercules, Agricultural Nutrition, Diamond Shamrock and Thompson Chemical. Martin made an application for a portion of the settlement in 1995. His case is still pending.

Art Diabo came back from Vietnam in June 1968 with a mangled arm. A buddy from the reserve barely recognized Diabo as he was wheeled into the orthopedic ward of St. Albans Naval Hospital in New York. "He couldn't believe how I looked," says Diabo. "I still had red clay and paddy water all over me. The nurses said that they weren't putting me into a bed looking like that. Until then, nobody had bothered to wash me down." He was taken to a washroom and hosed off. A barber cut his hair and a corpsman brushed his teeth.

From then on, his mornings began with teams of doctors discussing what to do about his arm. "One doctor told me that he could save my arm," says Diabo. "I didn't believe him because there was no bone there." The doctor kept his promise, although it took four years and eight skin-graft operations to save Diabo's arm.

Diabo spent months in the naval hospital before being transferred to a veterans' Hospital near his parents' home in Brooklyn. He was released from the hospital just before Christmas 1968, although he would have to go in and out of the hospital for a series of operations later. Before reconstructive surgery could begin, his infected arm had to heal. But heal it did, and the better Diabo felt, the more depressed he became. "I went through a course of remorse and self-pity that started in the veterans' hospital," he says. "I didn't want to go home." He was only nineteen years old.

He retired from the military in 1970 and spent the next year partying with his friends in Brooklyn. "The Veterans Administration was paying me 100 percent disability, so I had a lot of liquid cash," he says. "I don't remember too much from 1970. It was getting real bad, so I decided to come home to Canada to the reserve."

Diabo moved in with his sister and her husband on the Kahnawake Reserve early in 1971, travelling back and forth to the military hospital in the States for operations on his arm. A year later, he met Marina. They married and had a son, and Diabo's life started turning around. A marine friend gave him a job as a police dispatcher, which he kept for eight years. After that he worked for the minister of justice as a Native court worker for two years. Then things fell apart. Diabo turned back to drugs and alcohol. "I had a big pension from the VA and my wife worked," he says. "She knew what I was going through at the time."

The Marine Corps let Beattie process out in the fall of 1969, six months earlier than anticipated. When Beattie called his dad to ask to be picked up, he also gave him the serial number of several weapons he wanted to bring home. When Beattie arrived at the Halifax airport, he was whisked through customs and sent directly to the RCMP office. "When the RCMP officer heard that I'd been in Vietnam," he says, "he let me go."

But getting back to civilian life in Canada was a difficult adjustment for Beattie. "The weirdest thing I found was that after a year of being with only male company," he says, "you get used to using bad language. It was tough getting used to being back in public."

Beattie didn't talk about Vietnam in those early years, and no one ever asked him to. He remembers feeling uncomfortable around draft dodgers. "I didn't have anything against them because they left their country because the war was wrong and they gave up the benefits of the U.S.," says Beattie. "It's the guys who got out of service because their father was a senator or they faked an injury. Those guys get all the benefits of U.S. citizenship without accepting the negatives."

No one met Mike Gillhooley at the bus station when he arrived in Montreal at 11 p.m. one night in 1969, although he'd phoned ahead to let his family know when he'd be there. "I got in and no one was there," he says, "so I got drunk for three days."

After he was home for a bit, he realized he didn't understand his friends anymore. "At parties, I'd look at them," he says.

"I'd think, 'Oh come on, these guys are kids. They're acting like kids.'" After a while, Gillhooley realized that the problem wasn't them, it was him.

Gillhooley tried to talk to his friends about Vietnam, but they didn't want to listen. "All they wanted to hear was Rambo stories, but I didn't want to tell Rambo stories," he said. "I just wanted to talk to someone."

Gillhooley went to the Canadian Legion in Pierrefonds, in search of other veterans. When he showed the sergeant of arms his military discharge, however, the man refused to accept him. "Oh no, that's American. We don't take Americans in the Canadian Legion," he said.

When Gillhooley told him he was a Canadian citizen, the man was shocked. "Which war were you in? You're so young." When Gillhooley told him he had served in Vietnam, he scowled. "Oh, you're one of those baby killers. Get outta here."

After that, Gillhooley gave up on finding anyone to understand him. "I told myself that I better keep my mouth shut," he says. His silence prevented him from dealing with his past. After a while, he couldn't handle any reminder of Vietnam.

Gillhooley found a job in the data centre at Canadian Pacific Railway where he worked for three years before any of his colleagues found out about his military service. He liked the anonymity.

But one day a conversation with some of the guys led to a discussion about Vietnam. "I was sitting there trying to ignore it," says Gillhooley. "They were all know-it-alls. They didn't know what they were talking about." Gillhooley listened to the guys brag about how they'd handle situations if they were in Vietnam. All he could think was, "You'd survive, buddy. That's all you try to do." But he didn't say a word.

About a week later, one of the guys came into the cafeteria during coffee break. "Hey everybody, I've got some news," he said. "Mike Gillhooley's a Vietnam veteran." While drinking with some of the guys after work one night, Gillhooley's boss had let the secret slip out.

From then on, his co-workers teased Gillhooley incessantly. When he handed something to one of them, one of the others would say, "Hey, watch out, eh? He might have booby-trapped it." Eventually, Gillhooley couldn't stand it anymore. He quit his job to get away from them. And he kept trying to forget Vietnam.

Richard Malboeuf's military duty ended in October 1970, and he couldn't wait to get home to Montreal. As he stepped from the airplane into Dorval airport, he saw several Canadian soldiers holding semi-automatic rifles. Prime Minister Trudeau had just invoked the War Measures Act, but Malboeuf didn't know that. He instinctively reached for his M-16 before remembering its absence. He felt helpless. He couldn't help wondering if he had been smart to leave Vietnam. He had had no choice. "I had tried to extend for another tour, but back then they weren't letting you go three tours. They were downsizing then."

Since Malboeuf's DEROS (date eligible to return from overseas) was eleven days earlier than scheduled, no one was waiting for him at the airport. Malboeuf wanted to see his father but knew he wouldn't be off work for a few hours. He got into a cab and went straight to the Pierrefonds tavern. Even there, soldiers patrolled the streets. The cabby explained the situation in Montreal on the way.

Malboeuf called his buddies, but they weren't free until later that night. He had a couple of beers and went to his parents'. "I ended up waiting outside until my mother got home," he says.

Malboeuf didn't get the welcome he expected from his mother either. When she arrived all she said was, "What are you doing here? Why didn't you call?" When his brother and two sisters came home they had a family dinner together. "I was glad to be home," says Malboeuf, "but I didn't fit in. It felt more like a leave or vacation. I still had the urge to go back."

His family thought he was paranoid because he was obsessed with safety. "We'd go for a walk and I'd walk in the middle of the road. I couldn't walk on the sides," he says. "I was scared of the dark. The night time belonged to the gooks."

He also had a hard time finding a job. He considered the police and various security forces, but they demanded twenty-one-year-olds. Although he had two tours of duty under his belt, Malboeuf was still only twenty years old. While he was trying to decide what to do with his life he spent a month partying with his friends. But he couldn't understand them anymore. "A lot of the things they were doing seemed childish," he says. "They'd get excited over little things. I'd say, 'Relax, nobody's going to die.'"

He wanted to tell his friends about his experiences, but everyone talked about how wrong the war was. After a while, Malboeuf refused to talk about Vietnam at all. "I wasn't ashamed of myself, of what I did, because I knew what I did," he says, "but when people look at you with disgust… You know, I don't want to talk about what I did—am I blowing my own horn?—so I don't want to talk about it. But I was proud of what I did. I never backed down. I was not afraid. I've got medals on the wall."

Al Clause hadn't wanted to stay in the Marine Corps after serving his two tours in 1969 and 1970, but his superiors refused to let him out early. He had asked if he could serve his last five months on Okinawa, but they refused that too.

Instead, Clause was assigned to an artillery unit in California. "When I got there I asked, 'Why would they send an engineer to an artillery outfit? Where is the engineer equipment?' In Vietnam, we had engineers, bulldozers and generators and that, you know, to dig our pits and do this and that for us."

The marine handed Clause a foot-high stack of papers in response. "Sergeant," he said, "when the war comes, that stack becomes real."

Clause spent the 1970 Christmas season filling out paperwork while all his buddies went home.

After leaving the marines at the beginning of 1971, a resentful Clause returned to Canada and found the first of many jobs. "I worked in the mines in Sudbury," he says. "I was a grader operator for a while, and I worked in a quarry. I had about six jobs the first year." By late 1971, Al Clause had moved to London, Ontario, to live with his aunt and uncle. He found a steady job at Ford Motor Company in 1972 and that's where he's been working ever since. "I wasn't planning to stay long because I wanted to go to South America," says Clause. "Something happened and I ended up staying."

All the soldiers sat in a huge room, hugging their luggage. Someone had stolen one of Richard Legault's bags when he let his guard down, but he was more concerned about the small bottle of yellow liquid that was his ticket home. "They wouldn't let a GI go back home under the influence of any kind of drugs," he says. "You had to hold on to your urine test to make sure someone didn't switch it. I felt like a lamb among wolves."

The army made sure that soldiers who served in Vietnam returned to America sober, straight and clean. Before leaving Cam Ranh Bay, a soldier got a new haircut, a new uniform, even new shoes. He turned in any old uniforms. Then he exchanged his military vouchers for U.S. dollars. Before he could leave, however, he had to undergo urine tests until one came out clean.

It was August 1971. Legault still had three months before his three-year service was finished, but the army let him process out early. He flew home to Montreal where his fiancée was waiting.

As soon as Legault called her to say he was home, Nicole quit her job. "At that time, I couldn't take a month off," she says. "I couldn't function. When he came back, I weighed eighty-seven pounds. I was almost dying. My hair was thinner. Everything inside of me was mushy. All I wanted was to be with him."

A few days after Legault's return, the couple drove to a secret spot north of Montreal, bringing along all the letters they had exchanged during his three-year stint in the military. They sat in the warm July sun, taking turns reading their letters to each other. As evening fell, they selected a few keepsakes and built a bonfire. They planned their wedding while the letters burned.

For the next month, Legault and his fiancée spent every day together. They were happy, but Nicole could tell that something was bothering her husband-to-be. "Richard was very aggressive," she says, "even when waiting at the red light. He was frustrated with civilians."

Legault was upset at the lackadaisical attitude he saw in Canada. "People were living the good life while these things were going on over there," he says. "It was unfair that no one worried about that country. I didn't feel very much pride in my province or country for not taking part in that and helping to finish it as soon as possible."

Canadians were too busy discussing Prime Minister Trudeau's new wife and their country's new multiculturalism policy to think about what might be happening in Vietnam. They didn't care that U.S. planes were bombing Viet Cong supply routes in Cambodia and that the war had spread to Cambodia and Laos.

Legault couldn't figure out how to fit into his life in Canada. "My friends told me I was sort of lost when I came back," says Legault. "They had all changed and I hadn't seen them for three years. Most of them were hippies, smoking pot. I was military."

He also felt guilty for having left his family in crisis. Both sisters were experiencing major depressions when he got home. One of them had suffered a nervous breakdown while he was gone, and his parents hadn't told him. Legault felt as though he should have been there to help.

CHAPTER SIX

Hidden Trauma

Claude Martin knew that something was wrong on his first day back in the United States. "After my tour of duty, we landed at Alturas before going home on leave," he says. "Myself and a group of marines were walking down a street when a car backfired. Every one of us hit the deck." A similar dive in the jungle would have saved Martin's life, but in America it made him look and feel silly.

Martin couldn't sleep that first night, or any other night that first year. "I would wake up every two hours automatically," he says. "I could hear a fly land on a blanket."

When he did sleep, he'd remember moments in Vietnam that hadn't scared him at the time, but now terrified him. He saw Vietnamese bodies lying in front of him, some bloody and dismembered. They were the enemy. If one of those Viet Cong still lived, he'd kill any marine who got close enough. Yet Martin moved forward, over and past all those bodies. Push. Push. Push. In his dream, Martin carried a .45 in his hand as he walked. As he passed each body, he shot it in the head. Or he bayoneted it. If several were bunched together, he used his M-14. If they were stacked, he stuck a charge underneath and blew them up.

In Vietnam, Martin had been used to these situations. Some part of him had been able to block out the action so that it hadn't seemed real. Not all marines dealt with war so successfully. Claude Martin remembers that blowing up bodies destroyed a fellow marine. "This teenage guy always watched monster movies," he says. "The body parts went flying in the air and this teenager was lying in a rice paddy. When he got up, a hand was hanging right in front of him. He was wiped out. I never saw him again."

In his dreams, Martin felt like that frightened teenager. Every event became magnified and horrific. Martin realized that his senses were overloaded, but he didn't think he could do anything about it.

Martin didn't know it at the time, but he was suffering symptoms of post -traumatic stress disorder (PTSD). Veterans of World War I had called it shell shock. To veterans of World War II it was combat fatigue. Martin knew it as the Vietnam veteran syndrome. In 1982, health professionals in the United States officially recognized the condition as PTSD, and its victims included not only war veterans, but those who had suffered any traumatic event, including torture, rape, car accidents, natural disasters and explosions. PTSD was found to be particularly common among police officers, firemen and health care workers.

It was the work of two Americans, Dr. Khiam Shutan and Art Blanc, that resulted in PTSD being included in the third edition of the *American Diagnostic and Statistical Manual of Mental Disorders* (DSM III) in 1981. Accepting PTSD into the DSM was a huge change in thinking for American psychologists, says Matthew J. Friedman, the executive director of the National Center for PTSD in White River Junction, Vermont. "From a historical perspective," he wrote in a 1994 paper, "the significant change ushered in by the PTSD concept was the stipulation that the etiologic agent was outside the individual him or herself (i.e. the traumatic event) rather than an inherent individual weakness (i.e. a traumatic neurosis)."

To be diagnosed with the disorder, a person had to demonstrate three different types of symptoms: troubling memories in the form of daydreams, nightmares or flashbacks; the tendency to avoid or become numb in the face of everyday stress; and signs of over-stimulation, such as a severe startle reflex, insomnia, irritability and hyper-vigilance.

At first, psychologists also thought that symptoms had to last at least six months to be considered a problem, but they now realize that symptoms lasting only one month are still PTSD. They also added the most important qualification later—for a diagnosis of PTSD, symptoms must interfere with a patient's work, home or social life. PTSD usually occurs immediately after a traumatic event, but it can also be chronic or delayed.

Studies on PTSD have shown that the condition can be prevented or limited if treated immediately, but that didn't happen for Vietnam veterans. They were all sent home within a week of their tour. Even those who reported to American military bases to finish their service were not debriefed properly, although at least there they had other veterans to talk to. Canadian Vietnam veterans were worse off because they remained isolated for years after they returned from the war. The sole study ever conducted on them indicates that their isolation increased their susceptibility to delayed and chronic PTSD.

As combat veterans, Claude Martin, Art Diabo, Richard Malboeuf and Mike Gillhooley were all predisposed to delayed and chronic PTSD. If they couldn't deal with their horror, it would keep returning. It would cause dreams, flashbacks and an inexplicable rage that could destroy their lives. Martin, Diabo, Malboeuf and Gillhooley showed classic symptoms of PTSD when they returned from Vietnam, but they never expected the disorder to haunt them for the rest of their lives. They also didn't realize that returning to Canada would, in the long run, worsen their symptoms.

PTSD first made headlines in Canada in 1983 when Gordon Day, a Canadian Vietnam veteran trained in CPR, yelled for choppers in the midst of rescuing someone on a Toronto street. Day's flashback was a typical PTSD symptom. But it wasn't until 1991 that the first study on Canadian Vietnam veterans was conducted by Major Robert H. Stretch. Stretch studied Canadian Vietnam veterans while visiting Toronto for Washington's Walter Reed Army Institute of Research; his results were published in the *Journal of Consulting and Clinical Psychology*.

Stretch's study indicated that fifty-five percent of the Vietnam veterans living in Canada continued to suffer from PTSD, a rate higher than any comparable American group. In the U.S., rates of PTSD ranged from 5.1 percent for U.S. army personnel to 32.1 percent for civilian veterans. "The most surprising result was the overall prevalence of PTSD in Canada compared to studies I've done here in the States," said Stretch. "I think the fact that there were no loose associations of veterans like those in the States made it more difficult for Canadians."

Stretch also found that veterans like Martin, Diabo, Malboeuf and Gillhooley were worse off than American veterans and deserters. "Those veterans who were Canadian citizens at the time of their service in Vietnam," wrote Stretch, "have significantly higher levels of current PTSD symptomatology than do those veterans who were U.S. citizens at time of service in Vietnam." Such a result implies that the stigma attached to Canadians who went to Vietnam has put them in a more precarious state of health than their American counterparts.

Their plight isn't helped by a Canada-wide shortage of psychologists and counsellors trained to recognize PTSD. The veterans' groups know of only one—Dr. Frederick Lundell, senior psychiatrist at Montreal General Hospital—who is both a trained psychologist and a veteran with combat experience.

Lundell's name has travelled by word of mouth throughout the Vietnam veteran community. He's a World War II veteran and he respects Canadian Vietnam veterans for the choice they made. They in turn respect his professionalism. Lundell has been treating Canadian veterans for PTSD since 1973, before it was recognized as an illness. "I've been a volunteer on this for years." He doesn't take cases he can't handle and he doesn't charge the veterans for treatment. "If it's outpatient treatment, I bill the province," he says. "Serious problems go to White River Junction."

Many of the veterans Lundell treats come from Ottawa and Toronto, as well as from Montreal. "I might have fifteen patients on an ongoing basis and I do assessments on referral." The Vietnam Veterans' Council of Massachusetts recently awarded him a plaque of honour for his work helping Vietnam veterans.

Canadian veterans in other regions are less fortunate. Vancouver-area veterans must go south to the United States for treatment. For several years, Washington paid Dr. Hayyim Grossman to cross the border from Bellingham to help Canadians, but now they go to him. The Bellingham vets' centre has also just begun operating rap groups in Vancouver so that veterans with mild and moderate PTSD can help each other.

In both Edmonton and London, vets have trained their own PTSD counsellors. Edmonton veterans worked closely with Uwe

Erickson while he studied PTSD for a master's course, and since completing his Ph.D. on the disorder and finishing a work term in Montana, Erickson has been an on-call psychiatrist for them. London veterans started a support group for PTSD run by the Reverends Forest Newton and Keith McGibbon, who are themselves veterans of combat. Both have become accredited Vietnam Veterans of America-sponsored Veteran ' Administration service representatives.

A number of veterans in Toronto work with Dr. Klaus Kuch, a psychiatrist at the Toronto General Hospital's Smythe Pain Clinic. Although Kuch specializes in PTSD in accident victims, he also sees a lot of holocaust survivors. Kuch's experience treating Vietnam veterans goes back to the late 1960s when he was a student at the University of Florida in Gainesville. He completed his internships in psychiatry and neurology at a Veterans Administration hospital.

PTSD is the way that Vietnam veterans cope with their feelings of fear and helplessness, says Kuch. Sometimes it's a physical reaction, such as when veterans drop to the floor at the sound of a gun. "For somebody who has been in a lot of combat, especially combat at close quarters in the jungle, that is a danger signal," says Kuch. "It's quite involuntary."

Kuch says that treating veterans has to be done on an individual basis. When reviewing patients' symptoms with them, he concentrates on their strengths and what they themselves see as solutions. The treatment depends on the desired solution. "For somebody with sleep disturbance as the main focus," he says, "you might try relaxation training or you might try some antidepressants which improve sleep disturbances in some people. If fear is the main focus, you might try possible ways of desensitizing that fear."

Treatment often backfires, however. "The person just ends up just reliving and reliving the traumatic event without being able to do anything about it to resolve any of the issues," Kuch says. "You can usually tell. If they get a lot more nightmares, then it's not working and you back off."

Although Richard Malboeuf still involuntarily ducks or dives to the ground when he hears sudden loud noises, he doesn't believe he has PTSD. "To me, if you hear something, you go down and don't worry about what people think," he says. "I worry about where the noise came from later."

He also sleeps only four or five hours a night, but he's not sure that habit is related to Vietnam. "I'm involved in politics, I'm involved in all sorts of things," he says. "So a lot of things go through my mind. Is it that or is it just the way I am?"

He doesn't have nightmares anymore, although he still dreams about things that happened to him when he was flying as a scout on patrols. In one attack on Airborne, four people died from friendly fire, but Malboeuf isn't horrified anymore. He says his dreams are no longer nightmares. They're only memories.

Art Diabo has nightmares less frequently now, and they usually occur every May and June, right around the time he got wounded in Vietnam. He takes care to limit his stress then. He also tries to schedule deadlines and trips in the spring and early summer so that he's constantly busy and thoughts of Vietnam have little room to intrude other than when he expects them.

Mike Gillhooley used to wake up sweating and screaming at night, but he hasn't done that for a couple of years. "I don't sleep very well," he says. "I wake up early and that. But I do sleep comfortably when I sleep. And I never used to."

Gillhooley has been dealing with his memories on his own for years, but they've become less intense since his second marriage. When a memory haunts him now, Gillhooley can talk about it. "A memory is incredible—anything can spark it," he says. "A smell, a song. All of a sudden something clicks from that memory. I remember when I got slightly wounded, I had a nurse, I remember her perfume to this day. I don't know her name, I don't know what she looks like, but I remember her perfume. I don't even know what it was, but if I smelled it again, I'd know it."

Gillhooley also limits his PTSD symptoms by avoiding possible causes. "You have to be able to learn the signs that tell you you are going to have a problem," he says. "For example, if I know that the sound of firecrackers is going to scare the hell out of me, then I'm going to avoid being around where there's a lot of firecrackers on firecracker day. It's common sense."

"This is something a veteran has to train himself to," he says. For example, the smell of Vietnamese cuisine is distinct and Gillhooley recognizes it immediately. "We go down to Chinatown and without even looking to the left or right, I can tell my wife where the Vietnamese restaurants are," he says. "She's totally freaked sometimes." Gillhooley didn't enter a Vietnamese restaurant for twenty years after Vietnam. "I was very uncomfortable because I just thought of them as Viet Cong." He does go into Vietnamese restaurants now, but he always sits with his back to the wall. "It's not that I'm scared or anything," he says. "I just feel more comfortable if I can see what's happening."

Gillhooley believes he has his own PTSD under control. "There's two modes for a soldier," he says. "There's a diplomat, who can be a loving, caring person, which is a normal person like all of us. And then there's a warrior, where he's confronted and it's a dangerous situation and he's got to defend his life or somebody else's life. I think the key to surviving is to switch modes and know when to switch back."

Not all veterans have developed the ability to switch back to the diplomat mode. Gillhooley knows one ex-helicopter pilot who won the Silver Star for heroism in Vietnam. When he was in Vietnam, the pilot volunteered three times to rescue soldiers from an area under severe enemy attack. His chopper was shot up the first two times, and his superiors told him not to go back in. "I have to," he said. "Hey, it's a job and you're paying me by the hour." The third time he went in, he heard Charlie on the headset with his call sign. "I got you this time, GI," he said. Then the tail of his helicopter got blown off and the pilot crashed. The medic in the back seat was killed and the pilot's arm was mangled.

"He almost lost it," says Gillhooley. "Here's a guy who's on the razor's edge. He could go left or right at any time, and it's sad because the guy's a hero, but he's got many, many problems. He still sees his medic being blown away in the back seat. He wakes up at night screaming about that. I'm worried about him all the time, because I don't know what's going to happen."

Vets like this worry Gillhooley. "They shouldn't be on the streets, in my opinion, because they are very volatile, very dangerous and highly trained," he says. "Some of them are still living in Vietnam in their minds day in and day out because they don't want to get away from it."

Left isolated and untreated, veterans suffering from PTSD pose a potential threat to everyone around them. Often, the first step to getting treatment is making contact with other sufferers.

CHAPTER SEVEN

Mutual Support

Mike Gillhooley had no idea that there were other Canadians who volunteered for the U.S. Army in his area until he came across the Canadian Vietnam Veterans—Toronto (CVVT) booth in the Milton mall one summer day in 1989. When Gillhooley identified himself, one of the members said "Welcome home" and hugged him. That day was one of the happiest days of Gillhooley's life, and the start of five years of intense personal growth.

Gillhooley soon found himself chairing the CVVT prisoners of war/missing-in-action (POW/MIA) committee. The job gave him a life mission. "I want to bring one guy out of Vietnam," says Gillhooley. "If there's one guy who wants to come home, we're going to bring him home. And if they're all dead, if they were killed, we want to know that too…because that's called war crimes."

Gillhooley thought he'd have a chance to rescue someone that very first year. In 1989, while he was governor of Arkansas, Bill Clinton supported the "Team Falcon" mission to rescue Americans held in Vietnam. The plan was to send a team made up of Arkansas and Michigan vets to Vietnam to rescue POWs. Gillhooley arranged safe houses across Canada so that the POWs could be protected and receive medical treatment. He also recruited twenty Canadian veterans who were willing to participate in any way necessary with twenty-four hours' warning.

In the end, the project was a failure. Gillhooley assumes that the CIA blocked their success. "We had guys in Thailand, along with two Laotians ready to cross over into Laos," he says. "The

Laotians got lost and never showed up. We couldn't buy the necessary equipment anywhere."

The only memento of the mission and the $9,000 it cost Gillhooley's association is Bill Clinton's signature on a certificate assigning Gillhooley official goodwill-ambassador status for the State of Arkansas.

In 1993, Gillhooley set up a separate association to concentrate on distributing information about POW/MIA's left behind after all wars. He now runs four chapters of the Canadian POW/MIA Information Centre and distributes a monthly newsletter by mail and on the Internet.

Gillhooley's experience is typical of Vietnam veterans in Canada after they find others with similar experiences. Although each veteran takes something different away from the meeting, they all find strength in the knowledge that they're not alone. They learn to take pride in their war accomplishments. Then they find the courage they need to help others.

Individual efforts have created several networks of Vietnam veteran associations across Canada, including the American Legion, Vietnam Veterans in Canada, the Canadian Vietnam Veterans Association, the National Aboriginal Veterans' Association, North American Vietnam Veterans, Gillhooley's Canadian POW/MIA Information Center, and the Memorial Association of Canadian Vietnam Veterans. Some of these associations have added services and activities to satisfy the needs and desires of a growing membership, while others have concentrated on their original mandate, letting members create new associations to accomplish different goals.

The American Legion, with several chapters in Canada, was the first organization to welcome Vietnam veterans. It served as a haven for many, especially those rejected by, or uncomfortable in, the Canadian Legion.

Thanks to a short stint in his own country's military, Ric Pillage—a Canadian who served with the American navy from 1958 until 1963—qualified for active membership with the Royal Canadian Legion. His fellow members at the Richmond Hill chapter gave him a hard time, however, because he served two tours in Vietnam—one in 1959 and another split one at the end of 1961 and the end of 1962 (it was broken by the Cuban blockade). "They called me worse than mercenary," he says. "When they call you a mercenary, it's a goddamn joke. I could have gone to the Congo and made a goddamn fortune."

Pillage felt more welcome in the American Legion when he joined in 1974. The Toronto chapter wasn't very active at that time and Pillage wouldn't have bothered joining if the post commander, also a member of the Canadian Legion in Richmond Hill, hadn't asked him to. "At that time, there were only three of us—one from World War II, another from Korea and myself. It was called the Department of Canada."

That was the beginning of a very active Toronto command post, which really began growing in 1982 when Russ Hazelwood took over. Hazelwood had a personality that attracted people and he was a man who reached out to others. Pillage remembers that Hazelwood was the first person to visit him when he came home from the hospital after undergoing cancer treatment in 1982.

Not all Vietnam vets were as appreciative of Hazelwood's style, though. Rick Malboeuf joined the Toronto chapter after reading a newspaper article about the group, but stopped going to the meetings after attending a couple. "It was just too formal as far as I was concerned," he says. "It was called to order and we had to salute the American flag." Since Hazelwood's departure, the Toronto chapter of the American Legion has been run less formally by Canadian Vietnam vet Bob Windor.

The history of the Toronto chapter is indicative of how individuals have influenced the American Legion in Canada over the past thirty years. In the '70s, the American Legion chapters in Canada were branches of those in the United States. In the '80s, the Canadian chapters had grown into their own division with a command post in Ottawa. In 1993, the separate Canadian division was closed down (along with Ireland and Italy) and the Canadian chapters again became offshoots of the closest U.S. command post. American Legion chapters still operate in Calgary, Alberta; Hamilton, Ottawa and Toronto, Ontario; Montreal, Quebec; Surrey, B.C.; and St. John's, Newfoundland.

Other associations arose as Canadian Vietnam veterans began getting together for mutual support and treatment for PTSD. One of these groups was led by John Leavey, a clinical psychotherapist and Vietnam veteran who had spent seven months trying to readjust after a thirteen-month tour on a medical evacuation helicopter. Leavey's self-help brotherhood met in Toronto from 1972 until 1983. Although there were only fifteen active members, Leavey kept in touch with more than a hundred Vietnam vets.

In 1982 John Leavey got together with Russ Hazelwood, who was then leading the Toronto command post for the American Legion. Together, they organized a third group called the Canadian Veterans of the U.S. Armed Forces in Toronto in 1983. They made contact with a number of Vietnam vets who were involved in the Toronto shooting of *Unnatural Causes*, a movie starring John Ritter about vets stricken with cancer after exposure to Agent Orange.

Two years later, the American Legion group, Leavey's self-help brotherhood and the Canadian Veterans of the U.S. Armed Forces all merged into the American Legion and began holding monthly meetings. A contingent marched in the Warriors Day Parade at the annual Canadian National Exposition in September 1986.

Meanwhile, a veterans' self-help group in Montreal, which had been operating since 1983, was about to break apart. Jack Kusiewicz, a schoolteacher and pastoral counsellor, had started the rap sessions for Canadian Vietnam War veterans with PTSD when the wife of a Vietnam veteran in his congregation appealed for help for her husband. A story in the local newspaper brought Kusiewicz's efforts to the attention of the authorities at the Ukrainian Orthodox Cathedral of St. Sophie. They were not pleased. "The church," says Kusiewicz, "didn't like their parish being associated with Vietnam veterans." Kusiewicz quit attending St. Sophie's to continue his efforts with the Vietnam veterans' group, which had grown from two to fifteen after the newspaper article appeared.

Several Vietnam veterans as well as a number of Vietnam veterans' wives—including Claude Martin's wife Michelle—called Kusiewicz to ask for his help. Kusiewicz had taken several courses about the benefit of group therapy and thought the Vietnam veterans might be able to help themselves. He started a series of "rap sessions" with the Vietnam veterans and their wives, but he hoped that his personal participation would end quickly. "I didn't feel qualified to run the rap sessions alone," he says, "but I was hoping that a professional would hear about what I was doing and take over."

For the next year, Kusiewicz had Vietnam veterans and their wives to his home every Friday night to share their feelings of rage and frustration. Although many of the couples he saw still ended up divorced, Kusiewicz believes that his rap groups helped as much as was possible, and he's sure that the sessions made Claude and Michelle Martin's marriage stronger. "There was one couple who I consider to be a success," he says. "Their marriage is very strong. They did everything together, and they're the only couple still together today."

Art Diabo and his wife Marina, who are also still happily married, frequently attended the sessions too, although Kusiewicz did not really consider Diabo part of his rap group. "He never needed my help," says Kusiewicz. Diabo chose to serve as a resource for the other veterans and was particularly helpful when it came to applying for benefits from the U.S. Veterans' Administration.

The Disabled American Veterans Association in White River Junction, Vermont, officially recognized Kusiewicz's rap sessions, but he still felt uncomfortable running them without psychological training. After a year had passed with no qualified replacement in sight, Kusiewicz realized he would have to take action. He wrote a letter to the Canadian Psychiatric Association's monthly bulletin begging for help. After a six-month delay, the letter was published in April 1984.

No Canadians responded, but renowned U.S. psychiatrist Dr. Khiam Shutan (who had successfully added PTSD to the U.S. diagnostic manual three years earlier) saw the letter. Shutan visited Montreal to sit in on a session. "Shutan was amazed at the problems that were being handled," says Kusiewicz, "and he couldn't understand how all those people and I clicked." Shutan also predicted that the group would only last a few years and that people would have to be referred to psychiatrists one at a time.

Before that happened, Kusiewicz recruited fellow schoolteacher Jeannine Mannix to take over rap sessions for the wives while Kusiewicz continued with the men. Their combined effort did nothing to change the outcome.

When Shutan's prophecy came true in 1986, Kusiewicz didn't have the energy to start another group of twenty-five. Although he's still friends with some of the veterans he treated, he no longer coordinates rap sessions.

Just as Kusiewicz's rap sessions were winding down, a similar association was beginning in Vancouver. About twenty Vietnam veterans started meeting in January 1986, in response to an advertisement by Mark Klindt.

Klindt started the outreach group so that veterans could help each other deal with PTSD. Klindt himself once suffered so much he couldn't find the motivation to get out of bed. "I had a sleeping disorder. My PTSD manifested itself as nightmares and I was afraid to move," he says. "My GP got me to see a psychiatrist who was a professor out at the University of British Columbia."

The psychiatrist hypnotized Klindt so that he could start understanding his nightmares and begin dealing with the issues they represented. Once he could function, Klindt decided to reach out to other veterans. "I was hearing too many horror stories about people who needed help and couldn't get it," he told a *Washington Post* reporter. "I owed it to them to help them."

About thirty veterans responded to that initial ad, although not all of them joined the group. "One of the first calls I ever got was from a veteran who had served two tours in Vietnam and still hadn't told his mother," says Klindt. "He was one of those who wouldn't leave any information and I never was able to find him again."

Woody Carmack was one of the first vets to answer Klindt's ad, and he attended meetings at the University of British Columbia and in a local restaurant. After that, the two vets began working together to organize monthly meetings in Carmack's basement office. To attract more veterans, they placed a second ad. Several people responded and monthly meetings began in April. By September, they were ready to begin the long process of incorporating a non-profit organization called Vietnam Veterans in Canada (VVIC).

Today the VVIC is the most active association in Canada. Members meet, without fail, every second Thursday at the British

Columbia Regiment mess hall. To keep the meetings interesting, VVIC frequently invites guests. In the past, guests have included Veterans Administration (VA) service representatives, psychiatrists who specialize in PTSD, and speakers from various U.S. veterans' groups, including Vets with a Mission from California and Vietnam Veterans of America. They've welcomed everyone from a consul general of the United States to singer Paul Hyde, when he released his *Man Who Knows Too Much* music video.

American Woody Carmack has been VVIC president for seven of the last nine years. He's responsible for two newsletters, many of the guest bookings and the van that drives Vietnam veterans from British Columbia to the Veterans Administration office in Seattle for compensation exams. "We've learned over the years," says Carmack, "that if you do several things during the course of your business year, it really gets attendance up."

Meanwhile, Rob Purvis, a Vietnam vet in Winnipeg, was starting on the project that would eventually bring together the veterans' associations in Calgary, Edmonton, Halifax, Hamilton, Montreal, Ottawa, Toronto, Whitehorse and Winnipeg. He was planning to visit the Vietnam Veterans' Memorial in Washington, D.C.—and he was looking for other Canadian vets to go with him.

The idea had come to Purvis on Remembrance Day 1985 as he watched someone lay a wreath for Canadians who had died in Vietnam. At that moment, Purvis knew he was not alone, but he still didn't know who those other veterans were. He advertised across Canada requesting any Canadians who had served in the U.S. Army to call him.

Woody Carmack and Mark Klindt from Vancouver called Purvis right away. Others took longer to respond. Mike Ruggiero, for example, was given a copy of the advertisement by a client. "I was a body-shop manager working for a General Motors car dealer in Woodbridge," he says. "This customer of mine kept coming in every day to see his car. One day he came in and I was reading this magazine that had Vietnam on the front of it."

"What are you reading about Vietnam for?" asked the client.

"Because I was there," said Ruggiero.

The client turned around and walked out of the office. "About twenty minutes later," says Ruggiero, "he came back with a little clipping out of the *Toronto Star*."

Some didn't contact Purvis themselves. Someone from Toronto gave Purvis the name of Robert Beattie in Halifax. Beattie says he probably never would have gone to Washington if Purvis hadn't convinced him over the phone.

Paul Ferguson and Art Diabo called from Montreal, saying that they both hoped to go, although when the time came Diabo didn't show. He was in his "lost" phase then.

Lee Hitchins, from Ottawa, first heard about Purvis' attempts to get in touch with Vietnam veterans when somebody gave his wife a copy of the advertisement in the spring of 1986. "I put it away," he says. "I probably never would have called if that POW hadn't visited." At the urging of a friend, Hitchins had agreed to meet with an American who had been held in Vietnam as a prisoner of war. Hitchins' friend and the American POW drove from Ottawa to Hitchins' Smith Falls home and the three men spent the next eight hours talking non-stop about Vietnam. "That was the first time I ever talked about Vietnam," said Hitchins. "That made me look for that number."

Hitchins called Rob Purvis and asked for a list of names of other people from the Ottawa area who had called. One of the names on the list was Doug Carey, a Vietnam veteran who lived in Carleton Place, a mere twenty-seven kilometres away from Smith Falls. "He came over that day," said Hitchins. "We decided that day to combine media contacts and try to get people to share expenses on the way to Ottawa."

The two arranged a meeting for all interested Vietnam veterans. It would be held at 4 p.m. on August 5, 1986, at Little David's Deli in Bell's Corner. A newspaper article appeared in the Ottawa daily the day before.

Hitchins and Carey arrived for the meeting about half an hour early and started to worry. Several local media outlets were already setting up to cover the meeting and the two veterans were afraid no one would show up. They needn't have worried.

"Twenty or twenty-five people showed up," said Hitchins, "and the phone rang off the hook with people who couldn't come.

We had to hold a second meeting to find out who wanted to go to Washington."

In the end, more than a hundred Vietnam veterans from across Canada planned to join Rob Purvis in Washington, D.C. After several delays, the "Canadian Run to the Wall" was finally scheduled for September 1986. The Canadian Vietnam veterans would visit the Vietnam Veterans' Memorial during POW month in the United States.

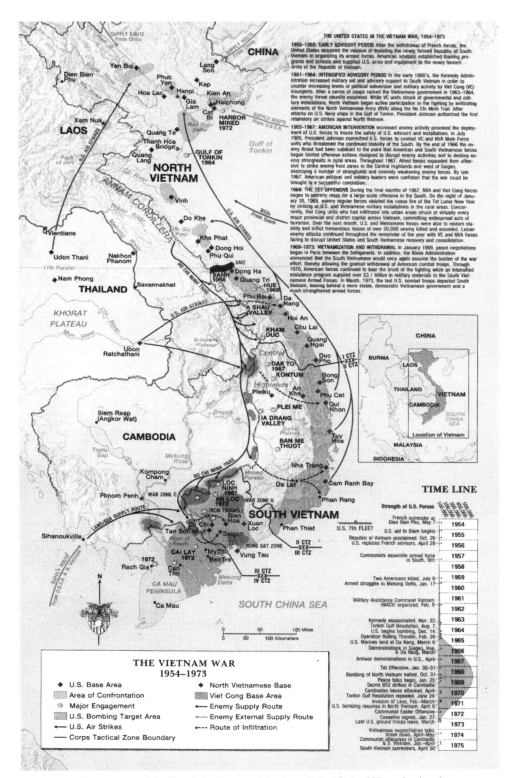

THE UNITED STATES IN THE VIETNAM WAR, 1954–1973

1955–1960: EARLY ADVISORY PERIOD After the withdrawal of French forces, the United States assumed the mission of assisting the newly formed Republic of South Vietnam in organizing its armed forces. American advisors established training programs and schools and supplied U.S. arms and equipment to the newly formed Army of the Republic of Vietnam.

1961–1964: INTENSIFIED ADVISORY PERIOD In the early 1960's, the Kennedy Administration increased military aid and advisory support to South Vietnam in order to counter increasing levels of political subversion and military activity by Viet Cong (VC) insurgents. After a series of coups racked the Vietnamese government in 1963–1964, the enemy threat steadily escalated. While VC units struck at governmental and military installations, North Vietnam began active participation in the fighting by infiltrating elements of the North Vietnamese Army (NVA) along the Ho Chi Minh Trail. After attacks on U.S. Navy ships in the Gulf of Tonkin, President Johnson authorized the first retaliatory air strikes against North Vietnam.

1965–1967: AMERICAN INTERVENTION Increased enemy activity provoked the deployment of U.S. forces to insure the safety of U.S. advisors and installations. In July 1965, President Johnson committed U.S. forces to combat VC and NVA Main Force units who threatened the continued stability of the South. By the end of 1966 the enemy threat had been subdued to the point that American and South Vietnamese forces began limited offensive actions designed to disrupt enemy activities and to destroy enemy strongholds in rural areas. Throughout 1967, Allied forces expanded their offensive to strike enemy held zones in the Central Highlands and west of Saigon, destroying a number of strongholds and severely weakening enemy forces. By late 1967, American political and military leaders were confident that the war could be brought to a successful conclusion.

1968: THE TET OFFENSIVE During the final months of 1967, NVA and Viet Cong forces began to secretly mass for a large-scale offensive in the South. On the night of January 30, 1968, enemy regular forces violated the cease fire of the Tet Lunar New Year by striking at U.S. and Vietnamese military installations in the rural areas. Concurrently, Viet Cong units who had infiltrated into urban areas struck at virtually every major provincial and district capital across Vietnam, committing widespread acts of terrorism. Over the next month, U.S. and Vietnamese forces were able to restore stability and inflict tremendous losses of over 50,000 enemy killed and wounded. Lesser enemy attacks continued throughout the remainder of the year with VC and NVA forces failing to disrupt United States and South Vietnamese recovery and consolidation.

1969–1973: VIETNAMIZATION AND WITHDRAWAL In January 1969, peace negotiations began in Paris between the belligerents. In addition, the Nixon Administration announced that the South Vietnamese would once again assume the burden of the war effort, thereby allowing the gradual withdrawal of American combat troops. Through 1970, American forces continued to bear the brunt of the fighting while an intensified assistance program supplied over $3.1 billion in military materials to the South Vietnamese Armed Forces. In March, 1973, the last U.S. combat troops departed South Vietnam, leaving behind a more stable, democratic Vietnamese government and a much strengthened armed forces.

THE VIETNAM WAR 1954–1973

- ◆ U.S. Base Area
- ▨ Area of Confrontation
- ✷ Major Engagement
- ▨ U.S. Bombing Target Area
- — U.S. Air Strikes
- — Corps Tactical Zone Boundary
- ◆ North Vietnamese Base
- ▨ Viet Cong Base Area
- ← Enemy Supply Route
- ←— Enemy External Supply Route
- ←-- Route of Infiltration

TIME LINE

Event	Year
French surrender at Dien Bien Phu, May 7	1954
U.S. aid to Diem begins	1955
Republic of Vietnam proclaimed, Oct. 26 — U.S. replaces French advisors, April 28	1956
Communists organize armed force in South, Oct.	1957
	1958
Two Americans killed, July 8 — Armed struggles in Mekong Delta, Jan. 17	1959
	1960
Military Assistance Command Vietnam (MACV) organized, Feb. 8	1961
	1962
Kennedy assassinated, Nov. 22 — Tonkin Gulf Resolution, Aug. 7	1963
U.S. begins bombing, Dec. 14 — Operation Rolling Thunder, Feb. 28	1964
U.S. Marines land at Da Nang, March 9 — Demonstrations in Saigon, Hue, & Da Nang, March	1965
Antiwar demonstrations in U.S., April	1966
Tet Offensive, Jan. 30–31 — Bombing of North Vietnam halted, Oct. 31	1967
Peace talks begin, Jan. 25 — Secret B52 strikes in Cambodia	1968
Cambodian bases attacked, April — Tonkin Gulf Resolution repealed, June 24	1969
Invasion of Laos, Feb.–March — U.S. bombing resumes in North Vietnam, April 6	1970
Communist Easter Offensive — Ceasefire signed, Jan. 27	1971
Last U.S. ground troops leave, March	1972
	1973
Vietnamese reconciliation talks break down, April–May — Communist offensives in Cambodia & S. Vietnam, Jan.–April	1974
South Vietnam surrenders, April 30	1975

Strength of U.S. Forces

U.S. 7TH FLEET

(Map courtesy of the West Point Museum Collections, United States Military Academy)

Clothing issue at San Diego Marine Corps Recruit Depot, 1963.
(Photo courtesy of C. Martin)

Platoon 380 lined up "asshole to belly button" for chow time during their first three weeks at San Diego Marine Corps Recruit Depot, 1963.
(Photo courtesy of C. Martin)

Above: Hiking to the firing range at San Diego Marine Corps Recruit Depot, 1963.
(Photo courtesy of C. Martin)

Above: Marine Corps Recruit Claude Martin during AIT (Advanced Infantry Training) at Camp Pendleton.
(Photo courtesy of C. Martin, California, 1963)

Left: South Vietnamese friends sent Jacques Gendron this portrait after he left their country. A note on the back says "to our friend Jacques with our kind thoughts and our thanks for your support in the common battle against communism and the red devils for threatening the freedom of our people."
(Photo courtesy of J. Gendron, Saigon, March 18, 1966)

Right: Jacques Gendron on the base phone.
(Photo courtesy of J. Gendron, Saigon, 1964-65)

Below: Jacques Gendron next to barracks at Tan Son Nhut Airport.
(Photo courtesy of J. Gendron, Saigon, 1964-65)

Right: Dead Vietnamese. This photo was taken by Gendron on a volunteer mission as gunner on a relief chopper.
(Photo courtesy of J. Gendron, Nha Trang, 1964-65)

Below: Jacques Gendron and Primo at Lyly Bar
(Photo courtesy of J. Gendron, Saigon, 1964-65)

Bottom: Russell, Audvason, Graham, Adams, Mike Le'Houillier, and Bob Beck at Tan Son Nhut barracks.
(Photo courtesy of J. Gendron, Saigon, 1964-65)

Above: A Buddhist monk committing self-immolation against the South Vietnamese government.
(Photo courtesy of J. Gendron, Saigon, 1964-65)

Left: Jacques Gendron and Jesse Barton in front of Tan Son Nhut barracks.
(Photo courtesy of J. Gendron, Nha Trang, December 1964)

A South Vietnamese unit leaving from Tan Son Nhut Airport.
(Photo courtesy of J. Gendron, Saigon, 1964-65)

A squadron of helicopters returning to Tan Son Nhut airport.
(Photo courtesy of J. Gendron, Saigon, 1964-65)

Street in Saigon.
(Photo courtesy of J. Gendron, Saigon, 1964-65)

A Vietnamese funeral procession on January 9, 1965.
(Photo courtesy of J. Gendron, Saigon)

Claude Martin changing a battery on a PRC6 walky-talky radio.
(Photo courtesy of C. Martin, Phu Bai, 1965-66)

Sikorsky landing on Hill 225, northwest of Phu Bai.
(Photo courtesy of C. Martin, Phu Bai, 1965-66)

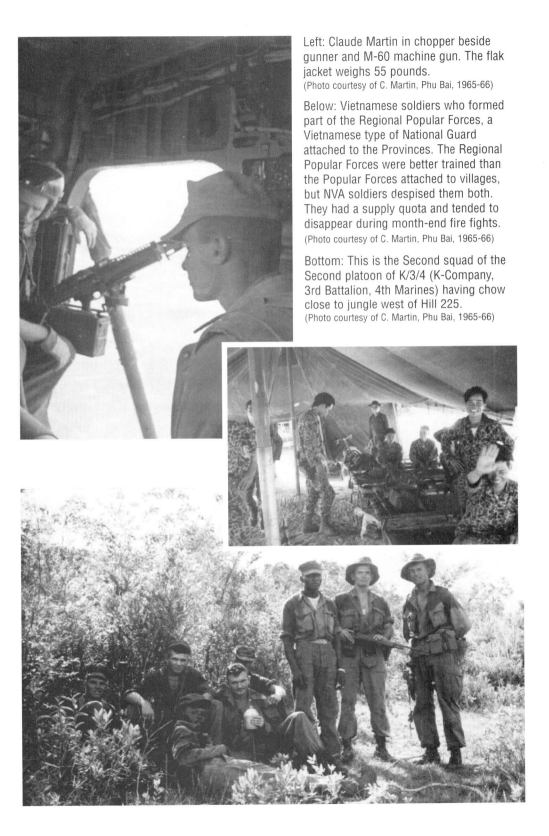

Left: Claude Martin in chopper beside gunner and M-60 machine gun. The flak jacket weighs 55 pounds.
(Photo courtesy of C. Martin, Phu Bai, 1965-66)

Below: Vietnamese soldiers who formed part of the Regional Popular Forces, a Vietnamese type of National Guard attached to the Provinces. The Regional Popular Forces were better trained than the Popular Forces attached to villages, but NVA soldiers despised them both. They had a supply quota and tended to disappear during month-end fire fights.
(Photo courtesy of C. Martin, Phu Bai, 1965-66)

Bottom: This is the Second squad of the Second platoon of K/3/4 (K-Company, 3rd Battalion, 4th Marines) having chow close to jungle west of Hill 225.
(Photo courtesy of C. Martin, Phu Bai, 1965-66)

Right: Marine Politz loading an M-14. Politz always said "there are three things that make men make mistakes: the unknown, the under-rated, and the unexpected."
(Photo courtesy of C. Martin, Chu Lai, 1965-66)

Above: Father Pierre Demers, a French-Canadian Jesuit missionary, at work trying to convert Buddhists to Catholicism.
(Photo courtesy of C. Martin, Hue, 1965-66)

Right: Claude Martin with three Vietnamese children who walked about 15 kilometres to safety. The Marines drove them back to the Hue orphanage.
(Photo courtesy of C. Martin, Phu Bai, 1965-66)

The girl in the photo of two children looks almost
identical to a five year old girl Gillhooley saw step
on a mine about 15 yards away from him.
(Photo courtesy of Bob Winder, Cu Chi, 1966-67)

Mike Gillhooley is the mortar-man in the centre. "Normally,"
Gillhooley says, "there would be sandbags all around up to
a certain height so that we would be protected in a pit.
This time we didn't have time to build anything."
(Photo courtesy of M. Gillhooley, An Khe, 1967-68)

1st Air Cavalry operations on the plains of Bong Son.
(Photo courtesy of M. Gillhooley, Bong Son, 1967-68)

The 1st Air Cavalry crossing a rice paddy, likely during Operation Pershing in the coastal provinces.
"Here is a typical view from a Huey from the vantage point of a door gunner," says Gillhooley. There
were door gunners on both sides of the Huey to aim for the tree line.
(Photo courtesy of M. Gillhooley, An Khe, 1967-68)

This is a typical hills people (Montagnard) village. The Montagnard tried to stay neutral but were forced to support the regional power, whether it was Viet Cong or American. According to Gillhooley, the Americans would stay and protect them as much as possible but "as soon as we'd leave the Viet Cong would come in and terrorize and kill them." Montagnards gave American soldiers brass friendship bracelets which inspired the POW/MIA bracelet.
(Photo courtesy of M. Gillhooley, An Khe, 1967-68)

The 1st Cavalry searches a Vietnamese village for Viet Cong, booby traps, tunnels or other enemy activity.
(Photo courtesy of M. Gillhooley, An Khe, 1967-68)

Top: 2nd/12 Cavalry rappels from Huey. The tree-line in the back is triple canopy, so nothing is visible from below or above.
(Photo courtesy of M. Gillhooley, An Khe, 1967-68)

Above: The 1st Air Cavalry landing zone.
(Photo courtesy of M. Gillhooley, An Khe, 1967-68)

Below: Here they just had a napalm strike on the enemy position.
(Photo courtesy of M. Gillhooley, Khe San, 1967-68)

S/Sgt. John Cogan, US Army, 52 Signal Battalion, 1968.
(Photo courtesy of A. Clause)

Below: The tree-line in the back provided cover for an entrenched platoon of North Vietnamese (NVA) soldiers who ambushed part of Arthur Diabo's company of marines. The dead enemy soldier tried to infiltrate the marine lines.
(Photo courtesy of A. Diabo, taken by radioman Michael Zang, An-Hoa, "Arizona Territory", 1968)

Above: Chowing down and writing letters in the field. (Arthur Diabo is third from the right.)
(Photo courtesy of A. Diabo, near Route 1 between Da Nang and Phu Bai, 1968)

Below: Michael Zang at his marine base in Phu Bai.
(Photo courtesy of A. Diabo, Phu Bai, 1968)

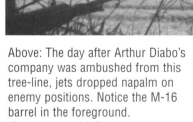

Above: The day after Arthur Diabo's company was ambushed from this tree-line, jets dropped napalm on enemy positions. Notice the M-16 barrel in the foreground.
(Photo courtesy of A. Diabo, taken by radioman Michael Zang, An-Hoa, "Arizona Territory", 1968)

Below: Richard Malboeuf in the jungle wearing a full pack.
(Photo courtesy of R. Malboeuf, A Shau Valley, 1969)

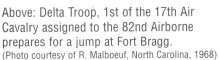

Above: Delta Troop, 1st of the 17th Air Cavalry assigned to the 82nd Airborne prepares for a jump at Fort Bragg.
(Photo courtesy of R. Malboeuf, North Carolina, 1968)

Below: Richard Malboeuf crossing a stream while on patrol for the A/2/504 for the 101st Airborne.
(Photo courtesy of R. Malboeuf, A Shau Valley, 1969)

Above: Landing on an LZ (landing zone).
(Photo courtesy of R. Malboeuf, A Shau Valley, 1969)

Left: Will Pitman (Pit), ? and Rodriquez taking a break on a hilltop overlooking the valley.
(Photo courtesy of R. Malboeuf, A Shau Valley, 1969)

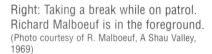

Right: Taking a break while on patrol. Richard Malboeuf is in the foreground.
(Photo courtesy of R. Malboeuf, A Shau Valley, 1969)

Left: Rick Myrice (right), Richard Malboeuf, and ? set up for night position in a tent made of three ponchos.
(Photo courtesy of R. Malboeuf, A Shau Valley, 1969)

Right: Resupply helicopter arriving on a firebase. The boxes are c-ration cases.
(Photo courtesy of R. Malboeuf, A Shau Valley, 1969)

Left: A Cheu Hoi (North Vietnamese who changed sides) demonstrates how he can infiltrate through barbed wire at LZ Sally.
(Photo courtesy of R. Malboeuf, A Shau Valley, 1969)

Right: A band playing at one of the LZs. The stage is usually a helicopter pad.
(Photo courtesy of R. Malboeuf, A Shau Valley, 1969)

Filling sand bags at Phuoc Vinh, III corp.
(Photo courtesy of D. Winrow, 1st Cav, Air Assault, Air Mobile, 1969)

Remnants of tracked military vehicle at Phuoc Vinh, III corp.
(Photo courtesy of D. Winrow, 1969)

Above: Tracer fire at
Phuoc Vinh, III corp.
(Photo courtesy of D. Winrow,
1969)

Right: Corporal Al
Clause holding M-16;
3rd Marine Division, 3rd
Shore Party Battalion,
HQ/S Company.
(Photo courtesy of A. Clause,
Quang Tri, 1969)

Bob Hope show.
(Photo courtesy of R. Malboeuf, Camp Eagle, December 1969)

Richard Malboeuf next to a LOH-6 helicopter (also called "loach" or "the elusive egg")
which had been shot up. The shell missed the pilot by
inches, went through the cockpit, through the back and came out the entry
compartment and missed everyone.
(Photo courtesy of R. Malboeuf, Quang Tri, 1970)

Danny Hine (wearing a confiscated North Vietnamese pith helmet and carrying an AK-47) and Richard Malboeuf (holding M-16) joking around outside their "hooch".
(Photo courtesy of R. Malboeuf, Quang Tri, 1970)

Richard Malboeuf (leaning on stand) and ? with a machine gun.
(Photo courtesy of R. Malboeuf, Quang Tri, 1970)

South Vietnamese money: 5 Dong.
(Bill courtesy of C. Martin, Phu Bai, 1965-66.)

The South Vietnamese Flag.
(Flag courtesy of C. Martin, Phu Bai, 1965-66)

Soldiers received their monthly cheques in the form of money orders to be sent home and these Military Payment Certificates for use in Vietnam. By avoiding greenbacks, the Army hoped to prevent soldiers from dabbling in the black market. They also switched certificates to force soldiers to turn in all the old ones.
(Courtesy of R. Legault, Long Binh, 1971)

Richard Legault in a jeep beside a 2 and a half ton.
(Photo courtesy of R. Legault, Long Binh, 1971)

The monument in Melocheville, Quebec.
(Photo courtesy of author, 1993)

?, Edward Semeniuk, ?, and ? during the Windsor memorial dedication.
(Photo courtesy of Yvette Emery, July 2, 1995)

The Windsor memorial.
(Photo courtesy of Yvette Emery, July 2, 1995)

Jacques Gendron's medals:
(Photo courtesy of author)

Anyone who served in Vietnam in the early years received three medals:
the National Defence medal, the Vietnam Service medal and a South Vietnamese Army medal.
The National Defence medal was given instead of a service medal because the United States
only expected to be in Vietnam for three months.

Later, the Vietnam Service medal was specially-designed for the conflict. The yellow stands
for race, the red lines stand for Vietnam (the South Vietnam flag was yellow with three
horizontal red lines) and the green stands for jungle.

The pin at the bottom reflects rifle marksmanship.

Who is he?
John Brown served with this Canadian.
His name was William and he was likely from Nova
Scotia. He was killed on October 4, 1967.
(Photo courtesy of J. Brown, Loc Ninh)

Rick Myrice, from Toledo, being macho.
Richard Malboeuf has been looking for him
since they served together.
(Photo courtesy of R. Malboeuf, A Shau Valley, 1969)

Above: Mike LeHouiller—a Canadian who served with Jacques Gendron.
Gendron has been looking for him ever since.
(Photo courtesy of J. Gendron, Saigon, 1964-65)

CHAPTER EIGHT

Lobbying for Benefits

September 20, 1986. Over a hundred men and women walked past the Lincoln Memorial and the Lincoln Memorial Reflecting Pool towards a dark corner with black granite walls. Most of the men wore battle fatigues or military uniforms.

They looked like any other Vietnam veterans' group visiting "the Wall" in Washington, except that each person carried a single rose, a Canadian flag or both. They walked beside the granite wall, each searching for one of the fifty-eight names of Canadians known to have died while serving in Vietnam. When they found one of the names, they set one rose and one flag at the edge of the panel below the name.

Thomas Edward Brown, rose, flag; Peter Norbert Bruyere, rose, flag; Gary Butt, rose, flag; and so it went on to Thomas Murray Williams, rose, flag. All Canadians. All dead.

The petite woman known as "Little Marg" placed a wreath in front of west panel seventeen. She looked down the list of names, stopping at the sixty-ninth line. Her son, Sergeant John Joseph Roden, had drowned while serving with the 5th Special Forces (Airborne) in 1969. Back in Halifax she had his Bronze Star, his Army Commendation Medal and his green beret.

Rob Purvis hadn't expected this pilgrimage to the Wall to attract so many people. Veterans had come from Edmonton, Calgary, Toronto, Kingston, Halifax, Windsor, Vancouver, Milton, Ottawa, Montreal and London. Some had even brought their wives. But Purvis was especially impressed by the two mothers. Margaret Roden had travelled from Halifax to represent her son. John and Pauline Wadsworth had come from Toronto to represent their son, Paul. Paul Wadsworth served as a U.S. Army paratrooper in Vietnam, but his name isn't on the Wall. He died in a car accident after he got home to Toronto.

Another mother from Chester, Nova Scotia, had called Robert Beattie two days before he left Halifax for Washington. She was the mother of John Kelly, a Canadian who was killed in Vietnam on February 15, 1970. Mrs. Kelly said that she couldn't go to Washington with the group, but asked Beattie to take a rubbing of her son's name from the wall. Beattie got a rubbing for her, and something else too.

While taking the rubbing of Kelly's name, Beattie met Eric Whyte, a Canadian Vietnam vet from Ontario who had been Kelly's best friend in Vietnam. Whyte had kept some of Kelly's personal papers and his wallet, and he asked Beattie to pass them on to Mrs. Kelly. Beattie gave Whyte Mrs. Kelly's phone number. When he contacted her, they ended up talking for an hour.

After visiting the Wall, Beattie, Whyte and the rest of the Canadian veterans, with their wives and the two mothers, listened politely to a speech given by Jan Scruggs, creator of the Washington monument and a Vietnam vet himself. Scruggs spoke to the mostly American audience about the Canadians and their visit. "The most important thing," he said, "is that they [the Canadians] will be energized by coming here to go out and find other Canadian veterans and start lobbying this [U.S.] government and the Canadian government for their rights."

The Canadians had already started lobbying the day before. They had met with American Legion officials and staff members of the congressional Veterans' Affairs committee to tell them how difficult it was for Vietnam veterans in Canada. Although they were supposed to be eligible for medical and educational benefits from the United States, they had run into numerous problems.

Several VA policies created difficulties for Canadian Vietnam veterans. For months, Mark Klindt, Woody Carmack and other Vancouver-based veterans attended rap sessions in Bellingham, Washington, every Wednesday because the VA wouldn't allow the counsellor to provide the service in Vancouver. The rap groups would last an hour, and then Klindt and Carmack would stay longer for training so that they could learn to help veterans in Canada without going through the VA. "It's a three-hour round trip, plus two hours down there," says Klindt. "And I was lucky; I lived in Kitsilano."

An American, Klindt was often stopped by the U.S. Customs agents at the border and taken inside for questioning, making his trip even longer. "They'd always ask if I was a deserter or something," he says. "So I started wearing my wings and they stopped bothering me."

The U.S. Veterans' Administration also refused to accept affidavits from Canadian doctors regarding the health of a veteran, forcing the veterans to travel to the United States to see a doctor or to fill out the forms that qualify a veteran for VA benefits. Charles Evans, the director of the Clinton County Veterans' Service Agency in Plattsburgh, says that his agency has been filling out claims for Canadians for years. "From my annual report of 1992, we had twenty-one Canadians," says Evans. "Most were filing claims for disability." The only difference between claims from Canadians and those from the U.S. is that out-of-country claims go to Washington instead of New York.

When the United States Congressmen in Washington heard about such difficulties in Canada, they were concerned. They knew that Canada and the United States had a reciprocity agreement dating from 1956. In part the agreement said:

> The Department of Veterans Affairs will furnish to discharged veterans of the United States armed forces residing or sojourning in Canada such medical, surgical and dental treatment...hospital care and transportation as may be requested by the Veterans Administration. The Veterans Administration will reimburse the Department of Veterans Affairs in cash for expenses...

Under the terms of the agreement, Canada's Veterans Affairs ministry should have taken care of all Vietnam veterans in Canada, but that wasn't happening. The Canadian government refused to pay benefits to Vietnam veterans, claiming that the reciprocity agreement did not cover a war in which Canada did not participate. The Canadian government also noted that

Canadians were eligible for free health care anyway and the veterans should use their country's health system as any other citizen would.

Many veterans in Canada, however, needed health care that went beyond standard medical insurance coverage. Those who had lost limbs needed wheelchairs, or braces or prosthetics, and not all provincial health plans covered these items. Some veterans had to undergo difficult procedures that were not available in Canada at the time. Art Diabo, for instance, had to travel from his reserve near Montreal to a Veterans Administration hospital in New York to finish a series of operations for the pedicle flap skin-graft that repaired his arm.

Diabo was already getting 100 percent disability payments by then, because they had started while he was living in New York, but other veterans who had been disabled by the war returned to Canada without realizing that they were eligible for payments. Ken Heatherington, who suffered back injuries and hearing impairment while serving two tours with the 101st Airborne, thought that his return to Canada made him ineligible for a disability claim. He didn't apply until after joining the Ottawa veterans' group in the late '80s. "Since then he's gotten benefits," says Lee Hitchins, "and he's taken advantage of vocational rehabilitation so he's taken a bachelor's degree and a master's degree. He now works as a social worker in Nova Scotia."

While in Washington, Heatherington and the other Canadians explained the difficulty Canadian veterans had in getting accurate information on veterans' benefits in their country. Many vets didn't know which benefits they qualified for or how to attain them. Others knew that they qualified for benefits, but weren't prepared to move to the United States to claim them. Richard Malboeuf, for instance, had wanted to become a pilot when he first got back from Vietnam. But the United States armed forces wouldn't pay for flight school in Canada and Malboeuf wouldn't return to the United States, so he lost the opportunity.

Art Diabo decided to go back to college in September 1984. "I went to the University of the State of New York at Plattsburgh," says Diabo. "I majored in sociology. It was close and I still had my veteran educational benefits." Diabo spent the first semester travelling back and forth from the Kahnawake Reserve outside

Montreal, but found that too difficult. He ended up renting an apartment in Plattsburgh while he completed his degree—which meant seeing his wife and thirteen-year-old son only on weekends.

The Canadian veterans encouraged the American congressmen to set up a veterans' outreach centre in Canada. The congressmen and Legion officials thought such a center would be too expensive, but they were fascinated to learn that Canadians had served in Vietnam. They welcomed the veterans and called them heroes.

It was the first time Canadian Vietnam veterans had felt respect from both veterans of other wars and politicians, and it energized them to expand across the country, just as Scruggs had hoped. "It was such a nice feeling over those two days," says Lee Hitchins. "We decided to start associations across Canada to keep working together."

Canadian Vietnam veterans' efforts help fellow veterans emphasize their unique problems to U.S. politicians. Two months after the Washington reunion, Robert Beattie's assistance to a fellow veteran brought the issue directly to the attention of a U.S. senator.

Beattie got a call early one morning from fellow veteran Rick Hazelwood. Hazelwood's wife had had him committed to the Waterville mental hospital in Nova Scotia the previous night. After an intense series of alcoholic and pill-induced flashbacks, Hazelwood had threatened to blow his head off. He had also kept ordering his wife to get down, as if he expected a bomb to land on them. That's when she placed a call to Waterville and asked them to pick her husband up.

Hazelwood had recovered by the next day, but the hospital refused to release him. They also admitted that they didn't know how to treat him. His call to Beattie was an urgent plea for help.

Beattie contacted the VA medical facility in Togas (Maine), which was familiar with Hazelwood's problems. They arranged for the Waterville hospital to transfer Hazelwood to them by bus. Beattie asked Robert Milne, a wannabe Vietnam veteran from Halifax, to accompany Hazelwood.

When the two men arrived at the Maine border and told the U.S. Immigration officer where they were going, he refused to allow them into the country. "The United States has a law," he said, "that says that if you have a mental disorder, you can't come in." It was 9:30 on a Friday night.

Milne called Beattie, who asked to speak to the Immigration official. "These guys are United States veterans," he said. The officer couldn't care less. Beattie told Milne and Hazelwood to stay right there in the lobby until he found a solution.

Beattie called the Vietnam Veterans of America (VVA) office in Washington and talked to Doc Raymer. Raymer couldn't believe the problem and contacted the senator for Maine. "I'm the senator for this state and this is ridiculous," he said. "I don't care who this border guard is; I'll take care of it."

The Senator called Beattie a few minutes later and told him the problem was solved. "I had to threaten that guard with his job before he would let those boys go over," he said. "I told him that he was to put them on a bus and get them to the hospital." The incident helped ensure that Canadian Vietnam veterans were not forgotten by the Senate.

The Canadians also initiated several stories about their plight in major newspapers such as the *Washington Post*, the *Los Angeles Times*, and the *New York Times*.

Although the Canadian veterans never got the outreach centre they wanted, their lobby effort succeeded in getting them the help they needed. Congress unanimously passed a law that qualified everyone who ever served with the United States military for veterans' benefits, regardless of citizenship. Ronald Reagan signed the bill into law on May 20, 1988, only a year and a half after the Canadian reunion in Washington.

The new U.S. law opened the door for the Canadian Department of Veterans' Affairs to assist the Canadian Vietnam vets. The six-person office headed by Violet Pannozzani actively crusades for all veterans in Canada. The office has assisted 4,000 Canadians who served with the United Kingdom during World War II, 300 who served with Australia, eighty who served with New Zealand, and forty-four who served with South Africa. The 1988 U.S. law added 2,400 American vets to its caseload. "Out of courtesy to the Americans, we have all the application forms the same as any Veterans Affairs office," says Pannozzani. "We even have American burial flags."

Although individual veterans can request assistance, Pannozzani says most of her cases are referred to her by the Vietnam veterans' associations and usually relate to disability pensions and quick admittance to U.S. veterans' hospitals.

"We have found that when any one of our groups contacts Veterans Affairs for a problem," says veteran organizer Robert Beattie, "we get an answer faster. As soon as she calls, it's like the paperwork in Washington is done, because Canada as a country is waiting for an answer."

Since 1988, the U.S. Veterans Administration has also made several changes which benefit Canadians. It has transferred all the Canadian claims to a single office in Washington, D.C., where they are processed as quickly as any other claim. And it has recruited Canadian Vietnam veterans like Rick Shannon, a Winnipegger who served as a medic with the 5th Special Forces in Da Nang from May 1969 until September 1971. He's been living in the United States since being discharged and now works for the Veterans Administration in Washington.

CHAPTER NINE

Mourning the Dead

Cathy Saint John just wanted to bring her brother home when she signed the official papers extraditing John W. Blake's remains back to Newfoundland in March 1996. Instead, she ended up fighting with Ottawa for the right to bury him in Canada's "Field of Honour," a veteran burial area in Mount Pleasant Cemetery in St. John's, Newfoundland. "I've taken away my brother's right to be buried in a national cemetery by bringing him to Canada," says Saint John. "I could bundle him up and ship him to California, but who's going to put a flower on his grave there?"

Canada's Department of Veterans Affairs won't accept Saint John's brother as a veteran because he fought for the U.S. military in Vietnam. "Vietnam wasn't a war," says a Veterans Affairs spokesperson. "So Blake isn't officially a veteran."

John W. Blake was nothing if not a soldier. He served as an Airborne Ranger in the 75th Infantry Battalion from 1969 until 1971. Blake was the first Newfoundlander to earn a Green Beret, but wore the Black Beret of the Rangers instead so that he could join his brother in Vietnam. He became famous in 1982 when he walked 3,200 miles across the United States—from Fort Lewis near Seattle, Washington, to Yorktown, Virginia—to garner recognition for the Vietnam Veterans' Memorial unveiling in Washington. Blake's toughest battle, however, took place within himself. Perhaps committing suicide was the only way to win his struggle with post-traumatic stress disorder.

While the Canadian government continues to deny John W. Blake recognition as a true veteran, the Royal Canadian Legion has finally accepted Canadian Vietnam veterans, actively recruiting them after years of rejecting them. To many Vietnam veterans, the Royal Canadian Legion once exemplified the loathing Canadians felt towards them. National Command in Ottawa adamantly refused to recognize Vietnam veterans as bona fide veterans, and it tried to ensure that Canadian Vietnam veterans stayed unknown.

Only a few chapters of the Legion were courageous enough to ignore national directives. A few of the smaller chapters—such as in Woodbridge, Ontario, and Beauharnois, Quebec—broke with Legion policy and accepted individual Vietnam vets as full voting members.

The Legion chapter in Kentville, Nova Scotia, defied a direct order from National Command when it decided to go ahead and include Dennis Richard Schmidt's name on a local monument to town residents who had lost their lives in war. Schmidt died in an ambush on August 8, 1966, while serving with Company E, 2nd Battalion, 4th Regiment, 3rd Marine Division of the U.S. armed forces.

Legion member Hal Jordan had taught Schmidt in high school and wanted his name added to more than eighty others. Jordan remembers local members being in favour of recognizing the Vietnam veteran, but it was a different story at the national Dominion Command convention. Fellow Legionnaire Gordon Maher recalls trying to bring the issue up as a motion. "The chairman of the convention said no, that wasn't to be brought up because they didn't agree with it," says Maher. "We just went ahead and did it anyway."

Kentville's bravado was rare. Until just recently, most Legion chapters across Canada not only refused to welcome Vietnam veterans, but also prevented them from honouring their fallen comrades at Remembrance Day services. Only Royal Canadian Legion chapters in Alberta bucked the trend.

Vietnam vets in Calgary have always felt complete support from the Legions in their city. "We've always been invited by Branch 275 out of Forest Lawn—a district of the city of Calgary—to lay a wreath at the Remembrance Day ceremonies," says Monty Coles, president of the Canadian Vietnam Veterans Association–Calgary (CVVC). "We've always been invited by the city of Airdrie to attend their Remembrance Day ceremony as well. We also lay a wreath at the main cenotaph in Calgary."

The Calgary Legion has supported Vietnam veterans in their city in several other ways too, including providing them with a room to hold monthly meetings and allowing them to use the Legion hall mailing address for inquiries.

In Edmonton, Vietnam veterans benefited from the same kind of support in 1989 when Randy Faires, Dave Herbert, Terry Kennedy and Rick Bott started the Canadian Vietnam Veterans Association of Edmonton. "At that time there was one in Calgary, one in Ottawa and one in Vancouver," says Faires. "We felt that we could extend our hands out more."

The manager of the Royal Canadian Legion in Edmonton wanted to help. Despite complaints from some of the Second World War veterans, he agreed to provide a place where the thirty-five members could meet. "The manager was excellent though the members were a little put off," says Faires, "but you learn to live with that kind of stuff."

The angry reaction that Faires received from a few Legion members in Edmonton was typical of many Legion chapters in other cities. In early 1987, Legion members in Winnipeg stopped their Cenotaph Memorial Fund from recognizing Vietnam veterans with a plaque; later that same year they went a step further and prevented the Vietnam veterans themselves from joining official Remembrance Day services.

A letter from the Winnipeg Cenotaph Memorial Fund to local veterans' groups in May 1987 started the turmoil. "We are researching the battle honours for the Vietnam conflict," said the letter. "A large number of Canadians served in the U.S. Armed Forces, some of whom laid down their lives. It is our intention to place two bronze plaques on the Cenotaph in remembrance at a later date."

Harold Bastable, secretary treasurer of the Legion's Manitoba and Northwestern Command, reacted to the letter with anger. He compared Vietnam veterans to those who fought in the Spanish Civil War and the Boer War. "The Vietnam vets weren't Canadian soldiers," Bastable told a journalist from *Western Report* magazine. "If you swear an oath of allegiance to Canada, how can you swear another oath to the American eagle? I'd say you're a traitor. You can't serve two masters."

Bastable wasn't the only Legionnaire who felt so strongly. When he raised the issue at the Legion's 33rd Biennial Convention held in Winnipeg in June 1987, all 348 delegates supported his motion directing Legion executives to prevent plaques honouring Vietnam veterans from being placed on the Winnipeg cenotaph. That precedent set the stage for a similar battle just a few months later.

The Canadian Vietnam Veterans–Winnipeg (CVVW) members, including president Rob Purvis, didn't particularly care about the cenotaph plaques because they hadn't been the ones to suggest them. They were more concerned about obtaining a provincial charter that would recognize them as a non-profit association so that they could join the official Remembrance Day parade in November. Legion officials had asked for proof of the charter when CVVW tried to join the 1986 Remembrance Day service. The twenty-two Vietnam veterans didn't realize that their new Manitoba charter wouldn't prevent a second disappointment. But in October 1987, the Winnipeg Remembrance Day Veterans' Committee—which included the Royal Canadian Legion, War Amputations of Canada, the Hong Kong Veterans Association, the Korean Veterans Association, and the Army, Navy and Air Force Veterans Association—decided not to accept Vietnam veterans into official Remembrance Day services. The committee insisted that the group needed a federal charter as well as a provincial one.

While many Legion members across the country agreed with the Winnipeg chapter's position, Jack Rabb, a Legion member in Smith Falls, Ontario, was disgusted. "Quite frankly, comrades," he wrote in his newspaper column, "I for one shall feel just a little less pride in being called a Legionnaire, until this travesty of justice is rectified.... Remember, it took us until 1955 to smarten up enough to allow the veterans of the Merchant Marine and Overseas Firefighters full membership recognition. The veterans of Vietnam don't deserve to be ostracized in this manner. They've already served their time in Hell."

The support of Rabb and other individual veterans across the country encouraged the CVVW members to devise an alternate plan: the Vietnam veterans would hold their own special service at the cenotaph on November 11 and then informally join official ceremonies at the Convention Centre.

An anonymous protester reacted to the news by dumping red paint around the base of the cenotaph the night before the Vietnam veterans' anticipated service. Luckily, a World War II veteran saw the mess in time to call the police. Firefighters removed every drop of the paint before the CVVW arrived for their 9:30 a.m. ceremony. Several people from the Canadian Armed Forces participated in the ceremony, and a crowd of eighty watched.

Meanwhile, organizations in Calgary and Vancouver had already been participating in Remembrance Day ceremonies since 1986, raising the ire of Bastable-minded Legion members, who complained about everything from Vietnam veterans in wheelchairs to the fact that the American flag was never lowered during a ceremony. The traditionalists who complained about the perceived disrespect wanted organizers to eliminate the VVIC and CVVC members from their parades.

The issue came to a head in Vancouver in 1989. "We had a guy in a wheelchair in our colour guard, and this guy in charge of their colour party (Sid Ward) made a big deal out of it," says Woody Carmack. "At the meeting for the year after that they were going to make a motion that we would be thrown out."

The Vietnam veterans called Bob Gillingham from the CBC evening news, and he took both the French and English camera crews into City Hall chambers. "That's the last time that they fucked with us," says Carmack. "Our group has been a member of the parade committee in Vancouver since 1989."

The Vancouver group has received other complaints since then—"We took flak from the Native veterans because we didn't fit in," says Carmack—but no one has suggested that they not participate in the Remembrance Day service.

The Quebec group jumped into the fray in 1993, when it decided to join the Montreal Remembrance Day parade and Legion officials refused. The veterans, at the urging of Massachusetts friend and supporter Bob Bolduc, considered unofficially joining anyway. In the meantime, Bolduc wrote to the American Legion headquarters in Washington, D.C., to ask them to pressure their Canadian counterparts.

In the end, the Canadian Vietnam Veterans Association–Quebec (CVVQ) received permission to join. Legion officials in Montreal called president Jacques Gendron late in the evening on November 10 to welcome Vietnam veterans into the Remembrance Day parade. Legion officials had two conditions.

The Vietnam veterans would have to be at the tail end of the parade behind all the other official Canadian participants, most of whom weren't veterans. The Legion also insisted that the CVVQ put their wreath at the side of the cenotaph rather than in front with all the others. Although CVVQ members complied, a stranger didn't. When the veterans returned to the Montreal cenotaph after lunch on November 11, their wreath was out in front with all the rest.

The following June, the issue of allowing Canadian Vietnam veterans to join the Legion was brought up as a motion at the National Command conference. Ottawa-based leaders didn't expect the motion to go through. They were wrong. Members voted in favour of allowing Vietnam veterans to join the Royal Canadian Legion as of October 1, 1994.

Another small victory in the fight for recognition of Canadian Vietnam veterans was achieved in June 1996 when the Canadian War Museum finally decided to add a small Vietnam war exhibit.

"There was never any intention to include anything in the War Museum about Vietnam," says historian Fred Gaffen, author of two best-selling books—*Unknown Warriors* and *Cross-Border Warriors*. "The upper people never considered the Vietnam War part of Canadian military history."

Gaffen disagrees. "Vietnam," he says, "was the locale of the largest number of Canadian citizens ever serving in a war in which their country was not officially involved."

CHAPTER TEN

Wannabes and the Quebec Memorial

The Canadian Vietnam veterans' fight for recognition has taken some unusual turns and attracted some strange wannabes. Jacques Gendron recalls an 1989 appearance with five other Vietnam veterans on the Quebec talk show *Parler Pour Parler*.

"In the end, the snakes scared me more than the Viet Cong," Yvon Roy told the audience. The five other Vietnam veterans stared at him in disbelief as the cameras rolled.

Then Roy spoke again, describing a patrol in the jungle and his reaction when he saw another American soldier hanging, caught in a booby trap in the trees. "I took my .45 and shot him to prevent him from suffering any more," he said. "Actually, he was a Canadian, Donald Morin."

It would have been a journalistic coup, if it were true.

Yvon Roy did not serve with the 5th Special Forces (Green Berets) as he claimed on *Parler Pour Parler*. He had served in Vietnam, but only for three months, not thirty-three. He served as a cook for Service Battery, 2nd Battalion (Airmobile), 11th Artillery from September until November 1971. By December, he was back at Fort Devens, Massachusetts, in the 67th Military Police Company—still serving as a cook.

"I knew he was lying," says Jacques Gendron.

Yvon Roy was a wannabe, Quebec's first and most infamous. Other veterans in Quebec were already familiar with Roy and his false claims to glory. Arthur Diabo had learned not to trust him. "He had a heart attack in the army and got discharged because of it," says Diabo, "but he told everybody else that it was because of wounds during a secret operation and that he was a spook. When you start talking like that, you leave yourself open to a lot of scrutiny by people, especially me."

Every Vietnam veterans' association across Canada has had wannabes—people who claim to be Vietnam veterans but are not, or, like Roy, claim to have served as grunts but were actually rear echelon types.

The Winnipeg group once even elected a wannabe as a president. The wannabe president got so caught up in his role, he filed a claim with the Vetera's Administration. He wasn't exposed until a VA representative flew in from New York to review claims for disability benefits.

The Edmonton group found out about their first wannabe when a new member, an ex-sheriff from Nevada, questioned another member's veteran status. "Unfortunately for him," says Randy Faires, president of the Edmonton group, "his girlfriend at the time actually told us that he'd done the falsifications of the work. We asked how she knew. She said that he actually sat at the front table and typed it right in front of her."

Wannabes are usually very knowledgeable about Vietnam, and those who actually served in Vietnam are the most difficult to expose. All wannabes bring discredit to real veterans. Some, like Roy, leave a trail of destruction behind them.

Roy's appearance on *Parler Pour Parler* was a good example of how a wannabe could damage other veterans' reputations by setting a sensationalist agenda. After Roy brought up the incident of shooting a soldier in the booby trap, another of the guests, Pierre Blais, began to talk about his attraction to young prostitutes in Vietnam, something that he probably wouldn't have shared under other circumstances.

Roy's claim that the man he shot was a Canadian called Donald Morin also led the veterans to include his name on the list of Canadians who died in Vietnam. In fact, Donald Morin was not shot by Roy. Lieutenant Corporal Donald Morin died in a helicopter crash on February 16, 1970, while serving with the marines. Nor was he a Canadian. He was born in South Burlington, Vermont. Although his grandparents had been Canadian, his parents and their children were born in the United States. But Morin's name is engraved on a memorial to Canadians who died in Vietnam, and its presence calls into question the legitimacy of every other name there.

Yvon Roy was a mixed blessing for the Quebec veterans. He knew how to get media attention, and that worked to the advantage of the CVVQ. He also dedicated a lot of time trying to get recognition for all Canadian Vietnam veterans. In 1988, Roy organized the first "welcome home" parade held specifically for Vietnam veterans in St. Bernard de Lacolle, a municipality next to the U.S. border.

Everybody got involved. A crowd of more than 200, mostly locals but some from New York and Vermont, showed up to watch. About twenty-five Canadian Vietnam veterans came from Ottawa, Toronto and throughout Quebec to bask in recognition. Robert Butt of Chateauguay was there in honour of his brother, Gary, who died in Vietnam on April 3, 1971, while trying to rescue the wounded.

The local Royal Canadian Legion chapter joined the parade, publicly supporting CVVQ's intentions to build a memorial to Canadians who died in Vietnam.

Violet Pannozzani, in her new role as Vietnam veteran advocate, attended on behalf of the Canadian Ministry of Veterans Affairs.

Military personnel from the United States were invited as well. A U.S. Army band from Fort Drum, N.Y., and a U.S. Air Force colour guard from Plattsburgh, N.Y. joined the parade. All the French media in Montreal covered the event. They reported it as an unqualified success, even after sitting through four different masses.

Mayor René Dupuis felt proud that his little municipality could help the veterans. Town council even renamed their main street Chemin des Vétérans in honour of the Vietnam veterans. Then Roy began to push for money. According to Dupuis, Roy demanded $2,000 from the municipality to enable them to have the monument. The council was not willing to pay and the monument did not go up in St. Bernard de Lacolle.

Roy took the monument to Côte Sainte-Catherine, Quebec. Within six months Chemin des Vétérans in St. Bernard de Lacolle went back to its original name.

Jacques Gendron had heard about the Lacolle parade and sought out Yvon Roy to see if he could help with a donation for the monument. If Roy needed money, Gendron was willing to help out.

Meanwhile, Roy had spent thousands organizing a dedication for the monument in Côte Sainte-Catherine. He decided to raffle off a camper to raise funds. He and Gendron registered the Canadian Vietnam Veterans Association of Quebec as an official non-profit organization with the Quebec Lottery Commission and printed a limited number of tickets based on the cost of the prize and a reasonable profit. Then Roy "lost" his set of tickets. Roy told Gendron that his son had burned all the tickets by accident. Gendron still doesn't know if that's actually what happened, or if Roy sold the tickets and pocketed the money.

Roy dropped out of the group, but he left the CVVQ with major debts and bad feeling from a lot of suppliers. Gendron didn't know it at the time, but Roy also hadn't paid any of the debts from the Côte Sainte-Catherine dedication.

That's when Gilles Sauvé got involved. Sauvé had decided to help the Vietnam veterans in November 1988 after seeing the St. Bernard de Lacolle ceremony on TV. "At that time, I had family who were Vietnam vets, cousins, friends and everything," he says. "I knew about Agent Orange and that, not much, but more than the guys here." Sauvé saved the association and in the process became one of five founding fathers, along with Gendron, Roy, Stan Blakey and Marcel Campeau.

After paying all the bills left by Roy, the CVVQ was in debt for $8,000. Sauvé came up with his own plan to raise the money. He knew that no banker would take him seriously, but he also knew he could get a good deal on a Harley Davidson. "I said to Jacques, 'Don't be a scrooge,'" says Sauvé. "'Sign for a $15,000 bike and I'm going to raise the money.' He wasn't really happy." But Gendron signed.

Sauvé kept his word and sold out the tickets for a draw at the end of May, raising $33,000. He's been doing it ever since, only now he raises about $56,000 per year. "It was hard the first year," says Sauvé, "because I just stayed with the bikers. But the second year and every year since, we've run out of tickets in March. It's a success."

Another supporter member of the CVVQ who works hard on behalf of Vietnam veterans is Dominic Rotondo. Rotondo is a benevolent wannabe. He wanted to volunteer for Vietnam in 1972 when he was only sixteen, but his mother refused to sign the papers. "John Wayne and the *The Green Berets* made me sure I wanted to go," says Rotondo. "It still hurts for not making it over there."

Rotondo has channelled his disappointment into the CVVQ. Since he joined as an associate member in 1992, Rotondo has spent all his spare time working for Vietnam veterans. He's written and distributed the Quebec newsletter. He's helped organize annual dedications. He's offered support to veterans considering suicide. He tracks down information about soldiers and marines who went missing in Vietnam. And he's led the landscaping and maintenance work at the Melocheville resting-place of a memorial to Canadian Vietnam veterans. Rotondo has earned the status of an honourary veteran.

Rotondo's dream, which he has now fulfilled, was to build a park around the Quebec Vietnam veteran memorial.

The memorial monument was erected by the CVVQ in Côte Sainte-Catherine in October 1989. There it sat—two black slabs of granite on an eighteen-by-twelve-foot white stone base with "Quebec–Canada" emblazoned across the bottom. One piece was a rectangle standing tall with a diagonal chunk cut out of one side so that it looked a bit like Alberta. The other rectangle sat sideways, like a large granite tombstone. The dedication read: "Vietnam Dédié à ceux qui ont servi, ceux qui sont morts et ceux portes disparus. Dedicated to those that served, died or are missing in action."

Five years later, Côte Sainte-Catherine town council decided to expand its town hall and told the Vietnam veterans they would have to either move or store their monument. After CVVQ members got a new site in Melocheville, they still had to build a foundation for the monument and landscape the site. That was when Rotondo got involved.

Rotondo, along with Jacques Gendron, Gilles Sauvé, Richard Davidson, Richard Legault, Ron Oulle, Peter Paril and René Demarais, spent every weekend all summer moving five tons of stone, levelling 400 tons of earth, spreading sod, laying masonry and building a concrete base for the monument.

Flowers were carefully planted around the monument to resemble the red, yellow and green service medal and the Purple Heart. Five flagpoles were raised. In the United States, three flags usually fly—the American flag, the state flag and the POW flag. Organizers added the Canadian flag and their own Canadian Vietnam Veterans Association flag. By October 15, 1994, the new site was ready for a dedication service.

Almost 2,000 people showed up on that beautiful autumn Saturday. Most were couples in their early forties and several brought very young children. A few wore blue jeans and black leather jackets. Others wore official U.S. military uniforms. Most of them wore black. Black helmets, black gloves, black leather, black everything, except the backs of their jackets. Some wore the black and red Vietnam Motorcycle Club crest. Police officers who served in Vietnam wore a dragon "Nam Knights of America" crest. Almost everybody wore a crest with a black head on a white background. The letters "POW/MIA" appeared above the head. "You Are Not Forgotten" appeared below. The men wear them for fellow soldiers abandoned in Vietnam.

The program for this memorial service was similar to Remembrance Day services across Canada: introduction, prayer, raising of flags, national anthems, laying of wreaths, playing of taps, declaration, remarks by honoured guests, special presentations, closing remarks and retiring of colours.

The two-hour service was sombre and quiet. At three o'clock, the stillness was broken by the roar of engines. Without telling anyone, Rotondo had arranged a low fly-by from two Kiowa helicopters stationed at St. Hubert. The crowd clapped wildly and smiled for the first time that day.

In the end, Yvon Roy's efforts to build a permanent monument to Canadian Vietnam veterans succeeded because others took over where he failed. Whatever the reason for his lies, his efforts helped establish Canada's first memorial to her Vietnam veterans.

CHAPTER ELEVEN

The North Wall

The man stared at the name etched in the black granite. There it was, down on the left side, between Randall K. Campbell and Richard C. William. He traced the letters with his finger. Larry S. Semeniuk. His son. Home at last.

After only six weeks in Vietnam, Larry Semeniuk was shot while serving with the 101st Airborne. It was January 17, 1968. His body was brought home to Windsor, Ontario, for a military funeral, complete with American flag draped over his casket and twenty-one-gun salute.

His parents were proud of him, but they quickly learned not to talk about their son to strangers. After the funeral, the Semeniuks had received crank calls from Vietnam War protesters who said they were glad Larry was dead and that it served him right for going to Vietnam in the first place. Larry's parents got an unlisted telephone number. When the army posthumously awarded their son the Silver Star for Gallantry in Action for saving a lieutenant from drowning, the Semeniuks kept quiet. Larry's mother died before the silence was broken.

Twenty-seven years later Edward Semeniuk finally got to brag about his son. Reporter Don Lajoie did a story on Semeniuk for a special section the *Windsor Star* was doing the week before the official dedication of a new memorial to Canadians who died in Vietnam.

At the official dedication on July 2, 1995, Semeniuk saw his son's name engraved with honour on a beautiful monument. He cried for the courageous son he had lost. It was the first time Semeniuk could share pride in his son's courage without a protester telling him his son's death had been useless. Semeniuk knew his son had died in defence of freedom and truth. Now everyone else did too.

The names of ninety-nine Canadians join Larry Semeniuk on the main eight-by-four-foot wall of granite. Right now, there is space for 204 names on the monument, but it was designed to include an additional wall. Estimates of Canadians who died in Vietnam run as high as 400.

The Canadian Vietnam Veterans Memorial, frequently dubbed "The North Wall," sits comfortably in Windsor's Assumption Park. Everything in this park reflects a dual identity, part American, part Canadian. Beyond a monument to soldiers who fought at Dieppe, for example, is a plaque identifying important buildings visible on the Detroit skyline. Another plaque, resting below the tree where it was placed in 1939, signifies a union between the Boy Scouts of Detroit and the Boy Scouts of Windsor.

When the sun sets, the light reflects an image of the Ambassador Bridge onto the monument's façade. When Joseph A. Bower built the bridge in 1929, he said that he wanted it to symbolize a "friendship of two peoples with like ideas and ideals." That friendship inspired Larry Semeniuk to cross the bridge thirty-seven years later to volunteer for the United States armed forces.

That spirit of friendship is also the reason for the monument's existence. It was built, ironically enough, by three Americans who forced Canada to recognize 100 of her own sons.

Ed Johnson and Ric Gidner, two Vietnam vets from Michigan, along with Chris Reynolds, Gidner's brother-in-law, built and paid for the memorial to Canadian Vietnam veterans which now stands in Windsor.

Johnson committed not only all his spare time and financial resources to complete the project, but also jeopardized his sight to finish the job, delaying eye surgery until after building and dedicating the Windsor memorial. It wasn't his first sacrifice.

Johnson had first heard about Canadian Vietnam veterans when he met a Canadian nurse at the Wall in September 1986. The woman turned out to be a wannabe veteran, but she piqued Johnson's curiosity. He remembered serving with a Canadian in

1969–70 with the 2/47 Mechanized Infantry. "During that time, it just never registered. I didn't even know what that would mean or where it was," says Johnson. "I mean, how many American lives did they save? I'm forever grateful for what they did."

When Johnson heard that the Canadian Vietnam veterans had never been properly welcomed home, he decided to do it himself. "So I organized a committee here in the Detroit area and I called it the Canadian Vietnam Veterans' Welcome Home Committee," he says. "It took two years in the planning and I personally went out and signed a contract with the Michigan State Fair grounds for $48,000."

That's when a friend introduced Johnson to Ric Gidner, who raised money and took care of security for the event. Gidner also signed contracts to bring the Moving Wall replica as well as entertainers and speakers whom veterans' organizations were familiar with, such as Tony Diamond, Chris Noel and Earl Hopper. Johnson paid for flights and hotels for all the invited guests. He had to mortgage his house to stay solvent. "The bills kept on mounting and I thought, 'Well, I'll get corporate funding,' and I kept writing to corporations," he says. "Meanwhile, I was draining what money I had putting things on charge cards."

Johnson's Canadian Welcome Home took place on the July 4 weekend in 1989, but it didn't go quite as smoothly as planned. The Vietnam Veterans of America (VVA), Chapter 333, which had initially supported Johnson's event, withdrew when Johnson chose the Michigan State Fairgrounds in Detroit over a similar location in Pontiac. Chapter 333 held their own Canadian Welcome Home in Pontiac the same weekend. They even sent a shuttle van to pick up some of the Canadians who had intended to go to the State Fairgrounds. Yet a third Michigan event, Freedom Hill, was scheduled for the same weekend.

None of the problems fazed Johnson. He was too overwhelmed by the positive emotional reactions he saw from the Canadians. He remembers one mother and daughter from Montreal. The mother brought the last tape cassette her son had sent home before being killed in action. "So while I was running around trying to take care of things, I wound up with this mother and this daughter and a group of Canadians," says Johnson.

"They played the tape for the first time and everyone was in tears."

The Welcome Home event was charged with small miracles. Johnson remembers the meeting of two Canadian vets at the Moving Wall. They had grown up together, gone to school together and double-dated together. They both volunteered for the U.S. Marines and they both went to Vietnam. And they were together on a mission when their chopper got hit. They were both blown off the chopper and each thought the other had been killed. By the time they came home from Vietnam, their families had moved away and lost touch with one another. When the two veterans heard that the Moving Wall was in Detroit, each came down to see if his friend's name was on it. They met while looking for each other's name.

"It's stories like that that motivate me," says Johnson. "When someone comes up with tears of appreciation and joy in their eyes, you can't put a price on it."

The Canadian Welcome Home cost Johnson $12,000 and Gidner another $10,000. It also cost Johnson his house, his credit rating and his wife, who left him the last night of the event. "If you love the Canadians that much," she said, "go marry one."

Johnson says he feels more bitterness towards his wife than towards the Canadians. "At the time, she had been going to school for six years, and I gave up a lot of our personal life to help her get through," he says. "This was something I wanted to do because I never went to school. I thought when I turned seventy-eight, I could look back at the papers and know I did something that made someone else happy."

It took Johnson two years to get his life together, but then he was back at Gidner's house with a bottle of scotch and more big ideas for the Canadians. They decided to create a monument to Canadians who died in Vietnam. They hoped that their effort would allow Canadians to separate the individual heroes who fought in Vietnam from the tragedy itself.

Ed Johnson explained their reason for building a monument in a seven-and-a-half-minute video, *The Construction of the Canadian Vietnam Veterans Memorial*. "In the marines you're taught to never leave anyone behind. There's 113 names on that wall and it's our goal to bring them home.... It is their right to go home and we are determined to take them home—and that's at any cost."

Johnson and Gidner began their campaign in earnest in March 1993 when their non-profit organization Michigan Association of Concerned Veterans (MACV) officially offered the memorial to the Canadian Vietnam Veterans Coalition (CVVC), an informal group which included all the Vietnam veterans' organizations in Canada. CVVC was led by Lee Hitchins from Ottawa and Mike Ruggiero from Toronto.

Lee Hitchins provided Ric Gidner and Ed Johnson with 113 names of Canadians who had died in the Vietnam War. In August, Gidner and Johnson went to the Wall in Washington to take rubbings of the names and verify spelling. Only 100 of the 113 names were on the wall.

In November, Gidner and Johnson had another meeting with the Canadians to discuss the project. The Canadian veterans, who included Lee Hitchins, Mike Ruggiero, Al Clause and Mike Gillhooley, decided to create a new non-profit organization called the Canadian Vietnam Veterans Memorial (CVVM) to raise awareness, money and land for the memorial. They began with a letter to the National Capital Commission (NCC), the organization which controls all federal land in the Ottawa region.

Meanwhile, Ron Mella and Don Sinclair from Vancouver took the issue back to their Vancouver-based veterans' group Vietnam Veterans in Canada (VVIC). To ensure that Vietnam veteran concerns would be represented properly, VVIC wanted all board members on the CVVM to be Vietnam veterans and they requested DD214's to prove it. They then presented the project as a special resolution at their annual general meeting. Although the resolution passed, some members were less than enthusiastic about the project because they believed that all money and effort should be devoted to veteran outreach programs rather than memorials.

Efforts to acquire land for the memorial did not go smoothly either. The NCC refused, suggesting that the Vietnam veterans ask the City of Ottawa instead. The City of Ottawa declined, saying that the "Memorial has nothing to do with the development of the City of Ottawa." This, despite the fact that they once accepted the statue of Colombian dictator Simon Bolivar under the same conditions.

The veterans lobbied hard to get the Canadian government to overrule the NCC. Letters went out to Prime Minister Jean Chretien; David Collenette, minister of veterans affairs; and Senator Jack Marshall.

Prime Minister Chretien's office responded in January 1994 by forwarding the request to Heritage Minister Michel Dupuis, who was responsible for the Canadian War Museum.

The bureaucratic run-around continued with Veterans Affairs Minister David Collenette's office sending a letter to Ed Johnson explaining that the Canadian War Museum land did not come under its mandate. It was the Canadian Vietnam veterans' first indication that they would get no support from the Ministry of Veterans Affairs. They had always known that some World War II veterans didn't want to be compared to Vietnam veterans, but they hadn't realized that prejudice would extend to political members in the Veterans Affairs office.

In the end, it was Senator Jack Marshall who took up their cause. By the end of February, Marshall had prepared a motion to the Canadian Senate to overturn the NCC decision and provide land to the Vietnam veterans. The motion included an official request that the House of Commons also look into the issue. Over the next month, Senator Marshall tabled petitions signed by 3,340 Canadians in favour of a monument to Canadian Vietnam veterans. Noteworthy signatures included three chiefs from the Eskasone Band Council from Nova Scotia; Bob Wood, MP; Carolyn Parrish, MP; Jack Frazer, MP; Bob Ringma, MP; Art Hanger, MP; Jake Hoeppner, MP; Philip Mayfield, MP; Dale Johnston, MP; Jan Brown, MP; Rose-Marie Ur, MP; and the Honourable Senators Phillips, Balbour, Comeau, Kelleher, LeBretton and Spivak.

In the meantime, land had been offered to the veterans by several private individuals, including Nat Stone, a farmer in West-Carleton, and Shirley Branson, an Ottawa resident with a spacious backyard.

Lee Hitchins, and Mike Ruggiero were particularly enthusiastic about a third offer of land in a cemetery because it included free landscaping and caretaking. The only problem was location. Capitol Memorial Gardens, at the junction of Highway 16 and Woodroffe Avenue, is outside Ottawa, in the Barhaven area. Johnson and Gidner went to see the spot for themselves. It turned out to be at the end of a two-lane dirt road and backed onto a maintenance yard. "We told them no way," says Gidner. "This was no place of honour."

When Hitchins and Ruggiero stuck to their guns about the Barhaven site, Johnson and Gidner considered revoking their gift. When Woody Carmack out in Vancouver heard about the disagreement from third parties, he got furious with Lee Hitchins. As far as he was concerned the whole problem was a lack of communication from the CVVM side. Shortly after, Carmack took over communication responsibilities for them, but was too late to prevent the impasse.

In April 1994, the CVVM decided to postpone the July 1994 memorial dedication to July 1995. In a letter dated April 10, 1994, they informed the other associations about the delayed dedication and described the Memorial Gardens offer with a quote from Ruggiero: "We do not plan to wait forever for government land which is why the offer of private land has not been dismissed." The letter did not mention that Gidner and Johnson hated the site.

Johnson and Gidner didn't find out about the delay until May, when they saw an advertisement for LZ North, an annual Vietnam veterans' gathering at Hitchins' residence that was scheduled for the same July weekend as the dedication. When they called Hitchins, he apologized and offered to pay for storing their memorial for a year while an appropriate location was sought.

After so much work, Johnson and Gidner didn't appreciate having to store their memorial for another year. By this time, Gidner and Johnson also needed help paying their bills. Although MACV, their non-profit organization, enabled them to raise some money, most of the $180,000 that it took to build the memorial was paid by Johnson and Gidner. "I took my $30,000 payoff for retiring early to put towards the memorial," says Gidner. "Then I mortgaged my house for another $50,000, but we went through that pretty quick."

On May 2, the veterans' hopes for a federal land grant were dashed by a letter from Michel Dupuis at the Department of Canadian Heritage to Senator Jack Marshall which upheld the NCC decision. Just nine days later, the *Ottawa Citizen* reported NCC plans to sell 1,500 acres in six "transportation corridors." The Vietnam veterans felt that this article implied that the NCC had too much land. Why hadn't they offered to sell some of it to the veterans?

On May 10, Senator Jack Marshall, who hates revisionist history, continued pushing the plan through by opening debate on his motion to overturn the NCC decision and provide a site for the Canadian Vietnam Veterans Memorial. He also advised the Senate of letters from the minister of Canadian heritage and the secretary of state for veterans affairs which both refused the monument because Canada had no involvement in the Vietnam War.

Marshall told the Senate that the letters lied. Canada had been involved in Vietnam. Marshall then listed all the activities the Canadian government did to support the U.S. military. "Canadian Commissioners shielded the U.S. chemical defoliant program from public inquiry.... Canadian aid during the war went only to South Vietnam and Ottawa stopped the shipments of ecumenical medical relief to civilian victims of the war in North Vietnam...," he said. "U.S. bomber pilots practised carpet-bombing runs over Suffield, Alberta and North Battleford, Saskatchewan before commencing their tours of duty in Southeast Asia... [and] Agent Orange was tested for use in Vietnam at Canadian Forces Base in Gagetown."

Most of Marshall's information came from Victor Levant, Canada's most respected expert on Canadian involvement in Vietnam. Levant detailed exactly how the Canadian government sold out to economic interests in a 1986 book called *Quiet Complicity*. The book details how Ottawa politicians claimed neutrality and ignorance to North Vietnam while Canadian corporations got rich off the United States Defense Department.

The Canadian government tried to block Levant's research, first by destroying a newspaper file on the Vietnam War at Lester B. Pearson Library and then by intercepting Levant's mail. Levant once opened a package of information sent to him by the U.S.

State Department and found gear manufacturer catalogues. Despite such harassment, Levant came up with astonishing findings.

"There was nothing we didn't do," said Levant. "We provided the food, the beverages, the military clothing. We provided the tanks, the trucks, the napalm, the Agent Orange, the TNT, the bullets, the green berets, the battle boots. We provided the casing for the bombs. We tested carbon bombing in Alberta. We tested defoliants in New Brunswick (Gagetown). The hospitals here tested pain thresholds. The universities were involved with weather transformation. We ran counter-insurgency networks at hospitals in Vietnam. Caring doctors and nurses went to help and found that they were part of the American spy network."

The United States Defense Department alone bought $2.5 billion worth of war goods from 433 Canadian companies between 1965 and 1973. These sales had sustained 140,000 jobs in Canada.

Not all of the senators were keen to debate Marshall's motion. Senator Philippe Deane Gigantès went on record as saying, "The fact that we manufactured Agent Orange here I would rather forget." But debate there was, and the Senate finally passed Marshall's resolution on May 31, 1994.

At this point, NCC managers assumed that the House of Commons would pass the same motion as the Senate did and overrule its original decision not to grant land to the veterans. They began talking to Jack Marshall about possible sites for the memorial.

On June 3, however, Michel Dupuis stood in the House of Commons and again upheld the original NCC ruling against the monument in response to a question from Jack Frazer, MP.

Four days later, R. André Gerolymatos from the Office of the Minister of Communications finalized the decision in a letter to Johnson and Gidner. A letter from Federal Public Works Minister David Dingwall was unequivocal: "No federal site will be provided for such a monument because the Vietnam conflict was not a Canadian war," he wrote. "I trust that we may now consider this matter closed."

Johnson and Gidner were crushed. Hitchins and Ruggiero were also upset but they wanted to go ahead with the cemetery site. Johnson and Gidner refused to accept the memorial site in the cemetery so they pre-empted any action by Hitchins and Ruggiero by writing to Capitol Memorial Gardens, refusing their offer. The Canadians were furious, but they didn't know what to do. They decided to delay the dedication indefinitely. Although they made their decision in June, they didn't get around to telling all the Vietnam veterans' groups in Canada until November.

When Gidner and Johnson found out about the new delay, they decided to withdraw their monument from the CVVM and go on their own to look for an acceptable site somewhere in Canada. That's when the Canadian Vietnam veterans' associations split, between those that supported Johnson and Gidner and those that wanted the Americans to place the memorial on the selected Ottawa site. In the end, only Quebec, London, Calgary and the POW Information Centre officially supported a change of location. The rest of the associations backed Hitchins and Ruggiero with their Ottawa site.

Johnson and Gidner started looking for sites. They considered Windsor, as well as the Peace Park in Fort Erie.

Many people assume that the London and Hamilton chapters supported the Americans because the new site would likely be in southwestern Ontario. That's not true. At least not in London's case. Al Clause and Don Winrow from London couldn't decide what to do at first, so they invited the CVVM and MACV to make presentations at their January meeting. Gidner and Johnson drove up from Michigan with a model of the memorial and suggested alternate sites for it. Ruggiero and Hitchins didn't show up.

Ruggiero and Hitchins got another chance in February, but they couldn't give the London chapter any idea of what their next step would be. The London chapter decided to support MACV and cut off all contact with Ruggiero and Hitchins.

Johnson and Gidner continued looking for a site for a dedication in 1995, so that it would coincide with the twentieth anniversary of America pulling out of Vietnam. The mayor of Windsor responded enthusiastically.

"It all started with a letter from Gidner and Johnson, two guys I knew nothing about," says Mayor Michael Hurst. "We started doing some research, because what Ric and Ed were trying to do had created a level of controversy with the federal government."

MACV's video and the letters convinced Mayor Hurst to meet with Gidner and Johnson. "I think that within ten or fifteen seconds, there was an agreement that we were going to go forward with this," says Hurst. "This was simply the right thing to do. There were no politics involved; it was simply three Americans showing care and concern and they were in an odyssey and they were going to bring these guys home."

The Mayor convinced Windsor city councillors to tentatively accept the monument in April, but the decision had to be ratified publicly on May 8. There were five presentations for the monument and five against it. Supporters included MACV, the Legion, a Canadian Vietnam veteran named Dan Newton, the city Parks Department, and the mayor. Those against the monument opposed it because they thought it would glamorize the Vietnam War.

Mike Gillhooley from the Canadian POW/MIA Information Centre attended the council meeting and thought Johnson and Gidner presented their case with panache. "The protesters went through their negative things before Ed Johnson spoke," he says. "Ed said to them, 'Aren't you guys glad you have the freedom to speak out in an auditorium? You can thank your vets for that.' Then he walked away."

In the end, the councillors voted to accept the memorial as long as it included the words "This memorial is placed here to commemorate Canadians who died in the Vietnam tragedy. It is not intended as a political statement concerning the merits of this or any other foreign conflict."

The Americans agreed to the condition. But there was one final sticking point. One of the councillors looked at the poem on the memorial brochure and said, "This poem is too political. We don't want anything political about the Vietnam memorial. Do you have another poem?"

Gidner and Johnson actually breathed a sigh of relief, because the poem on the brochure was Richard Malboeuf's. Malboeuf had decided to reserve his poem for the national monument that Hitchins and Ruggiero were still trying to build.

Gidner responded by tapping Johnson on the shoulder. "So,

Ed, do you have a poem?" Johnson came up with an acceptable replacement on the spot: "As long as we live, you will live. As long as we live, you will be remembered. As long as we live, you will be loved."

The Windsor councillors voted to accept the memorial. The dedication was set for July 2, less than a month away. "If you told me this time last year that by July first there would be a monument, I wouldn't have believed it," said Don Sadler, the Parks Department official who was in charge of getting the site prepared for Windsor. "Where there's a will, there's a way. Everybody got on side of this, and it happened."

Gidner, Johnson, Gillhooley, Ric Pillage and several other veterans spent Canada Day 1995 polishing the brass on the Windsor memorial. They were proud to have helped create the sixth monument to honour Canadians who died in Vietnam.

The Windsor memorial joined the Canadian memorials in Quebec and Kentville, as well as a third monument on the Canadian Forces Base Val Cartier, just outside Quebec City, to Charles-Eugène Laviolette, one of four Canadians who died with Canadian peacekeeping forces in Vietnam.

There are also two memorials in the United States which honour Canadian Vietnam veterans who served with the United States armed forces. One is the grave site of Michael Francis Campbell at Whidbey Island in Washington state. In September 1989, the Vietnam Veterans in Canada (VVIC) group from Vancouver placed a plaque on Campbell's grave honouring the memory of Canadian-citizen veterans of the Vietnam War.

The second U.S. memorial, in Albany, New York, includes the name of Canadian Donald P. Davies. The Albany people debated taking his name off when they found out he was Canadian. Instead, they left Davies' name on the monument in tribute to all Canadian Vietnam vets.

On Saturday July 2, 1995, Gidner and Johnson proudly led sixty-five Canadian Vietnam veterans and a parade of supporters from associations across North America along Riverside Drive and down to Assumption Park where the Windsor monument rests.

The flags were the first thing the Canadian vets saw. The Canadian flag, donated by Bob Windor of the American Legion, and the American flag were visible first, side by side, flapping freely in the wind. Then the black POW flag donated by Mike Gillhooley appeared, like a dark shadow aptly symbolizing the lies it represents. The covered memorial came into view last.

Master of Ceremonies Mike Gillhooley welcomed everyone and began introducing the speakers. Mayor Michael Hurst spoke first and talked about "neighbours helping neighbours."

In a moving speech, then ex-Senator Jack Marshall said, "The Canadian Vietnam veterans' sacrifice has not been truly recognized until today."

At that moment, Ric Gidner thought of a phone call he'd received the week before. Margaret Vidler, the mother of one of the boys whose name was listed on the wall, called to say that she couldn't attend the dedication. She wanted to make sure that her son Murray was listed on the wall. Gidner was thrilled to confirm that it was.

"It's for people like Edward and Margaret that we did it," says Ric Gidner. "They deserve to know that their sons didn't die in vain."

CHAPTER TWELVE

Memories

The American veteran clutched the small gold and purple heart in his fist and thought once more about the men who didn't make it home. Until this day, Michael O'Rourke had kept his Purple Heart handy in a dresser drawer. "I liked to take it out from time to time," he says, "and remember the faces of soldiers who died." He held it for the last time on November 11, 1995.

It was cold that day in Windsor, and so windy that O'Rourke almost lost his balance as he stood on a ladder next to "The North Wall." He held the medal above the cavity between the two granite segments of the largest panel as he spoke. "All monuments are steel and granite and they have no feeling, but the Purple Heart brings feeling into the wall," said O'Rourke, and then dropped his medal into the cavity. "It's there to be a beating heart for the guys who died there [in Vietnam] and for those who haven't come back yet."

O'Rourke's Purple Heart is the only memento left at the Windsor memorial that will never be seen again. The Vietnam veterans are collecting all the other personal items beside both the Windsor and Quebec monuments, in the hope of eventually displaying them somewhere. They are following a tradition that began at the Vietnam Veterans' Memorial in Washington D.C. in 1982. Park rangers there have collected more than 40,000 mementos, including a copy of the film *In Country* by Canadian director/producer Norman Jewison, several maple leaf pins and other obviously Canadian items.

Canadians began their own collection with an empty Budweiser can left at the Quebec memorial by an American trucker in 1993. Since then, several people have left donations in a mood of reconciliation, to heal themselves and forgive others. A draft dodger who originally protested the Windsor memorial, for example, left the first vase of flowers at the Windsor site. He made a point of giving it directly to Vietnam veterans who were cleaning the memorial the day before the official dedication. "These are for you," he said as he handed the flowers to Rick Pillage, one of the veterans cleaning the brass. "I'm a deserter and a protester but I'm sorry. This is the right thing to do."

Joseph Petraglia was so moved after the Quebec Remembrance Day parade, he donated a lighter to the collection of Canadian artifacts. The lighter inscription reads: "196th LF INF BDE [Lightfield Infantry Brigade], Chu Lai, Vietnam '67-'68 LZ [Landing Zone] BALDY, Vietnam '68."

People who leave these items tend to relive their own experiences. Karin Smith, for example, grimaced as she and her husband Gary left a wreath and card that said: "MIA/POW; Your sacrifice is not in vain; Your courage will not be forgotten; We will keep the faith; So that you may return again." She knew exactly how the families of people who went missing or died in Vietnam felt not knowing what had happened to their sons or brothers. For years she thought her brother Mike Gillhooley had died. They had only found each other a few months before this November day.

Gillhooley wasn't actually Smith's brother, but that's how she thought of him. When she was fifteen years old, Smith had written a letter to an anonymous soldier in Vietnam in response to a notice in *Teen* magazine. The military gave the Canadian pen-pal letter to Gillhooley because he rarely got mail from anyone else.

Gillhooley's response in February 1968 led to two years of correspondence between the two that ended with Gillhooley's term in Vietnam. Smith's final letter said that she understood that Gillhooley might not want to meet her in person after he got home and that was fine as long as Gillhooley let her know he got home okay. He never responded.

"I got in contact with the Canadian forces and they told me he would have been with the American forces to be there," says

Smith. "I wrote to the American forces and they wouldn't tell me anything because I wasn't a blood relative."

Every time her airline attendant job brought her to Montreal, Smith would check the phone book for Gillhooley's name. "Over the years, I've had friends check the Wall in Washington," she says. "I have a friend who's in the Canadian Forces and I had him check here to see if he was in the Canadians Forces anywhere." During all this time, Gillhooley was living outside of Toronto, mere miles from Smith's home.

"I never dreamed of checking around me," says Smith. "I used to live in Mississauga. He lived three blocks away for three years. I never dreamed of looking in the Toronto phone book. And in Milton, he lives on the same street as one of my best friends."

She finally saw an article about Gillhooley in the *Kitchener-Waterloo Record* in 1995. "The article said Mike Gillhooley from Hamilton," says Smith. "So I phoned Hamilton information and they only had one number and it was spelled wrong. It was some poor little old lady who didn't have a clue what I was talking about."

The article also mentioned John Cogan, from London. "So I phoned London information and got his number," says Smith. "This was around noon, and I was late reading the paper so it was the next day already. His wife answered the phone and said he wasn't home right then. So I explained the story to her—she got all choked up and began to cry. She said, 'Well, you've got to phone back at such and such a time. John will be back.'"

"So I phoned back and he was there. So I said, 'Does he look like this?' I only had one picture—and it was when he was twenty-one years old and now he's forty-seven so he looks a bit different."

"He sounds like it could be," said John Cogan. "Do you want his phone number?"

"I just about dropped the phone," says Smith. "I didn't want to ask, because I didn't want him to say no. He offered it right away."

"So I didn't even think. I immediately hung up the phone and dialled Mike's number and Julie answered the phone."

"I said, 'I'm looking for Mike Gillhooley.' He wasn't taking calls that day. But she just felt she had to give him the phone and he came and said hello."

"Is your middle name Patrick?"

"Yes."

"I just broke into tears and said, 'Oh my God, you're alive.' And he said, 'Yes, the last time I looked.'"

"That wasn't really the way I wanted to do it," says Smith. "So I explained who I was and he said, 'Oh my God, oh my God.'"

"So he's crying and I'm crying. My little boy's wondering what's going on. So I had to explain it to him and he thought that was so neat he had to go running down to my husband and said 'Mommy's soldier is alive. Mommy's soldier's still alive.'"

"So the following Saturday, only a couple of days later, we went and had a barbecue with them and met them. And we've been getting together since then," says Smith. "Mike's literally my brother. We've adopted each other."

Smith and her husband, Gary, went to the Windsor monument to celebrate Remembrance Day with Mike and Julie Gillhooley. Gillhooley introduced Smith as his sister.

After Smith and her husband laid their wreath beside the monument, they stood back to watch Dorilla Bastarache and Bob Bolduc lay a wreath for Fidèle Bastarache.

Bolduc had spent three nights preparing the wreath to commemorate the Canadian who had died in Vietnam on May 27, 1969. He wanted to honour the soldier who once shared Bolduc's home town, Gardner, Massachusetts. Fidèle Bastarache's father had moved his wife and seven children from New Brunswick to Massachusetts in 1962 for a job building furniture. When he was drafted for Vietnam four years later, Fidèle chose to comply, although his mother tried to convince him to return to Canada. He served eleven months of his tour before being killed in a mortar attack in 1968 at the age of twenty-two. He had been decorated four times for heroism.

Bolduc took care to place all the important items about Fidèle on his wreath: a photograph, a newspaper article, plus the crests of several Massachusetts organizations who made contributions to the Canadian Vietnam veterans' monuments in the name of

Fidèle Bastarache. "That was my way of letting his spirit know that these organizations remembered him," says Bolduc.

Bolduc was the one who had made sure the organizations recognized Bastarache in the first place. After Bolduc found Bastarache's mother Helen and his sister Dorilla in 1993, he went on a mission to tell Massachusetts politicians about Fidèle Bastarache.

Worcester (Massachusetts) mayor Jordan Levy responded to the story by giving the Canadian Vietnam veterans Lee Hitchins and Mike Ruggiero a key to his city "as a symbol of perpetual welcome to all Canadian Vietnam veterans." The mayor presented the key to the Canadians on December 23, 1993.

Massachusetts senator John F. Kerry's fifth birthday celebration at Boston's Copely Plaza Hotel provided an opportunity for Bolduc to present Fidèle Bastarache's story to him. Bolduc introduced Dorilla Bastarache to the senator during the December 1993 event. Senator Kerry was moved enough by the meeting that he offered to sponsor a resolution honouring the Canadian Vietnam veterans in time for a memorial ceremony scheduled for July 9, 1994. Senator Kerry's proclamation says in part: "recognition will at last be granted to those brave and unselfish individuals who made the ultimate sacrifice by the giving of their lives."

Bolduc's next stop: Senator Edward Kennedy. Bolduc persuaded Kennedy to sponsor a resolution on behalf of the Canadians that was read into Washington's Congressional Record on January 27, 1994. "This memorial will be a fitting tribute to the courageous young men and women who sacrificed their lives serving as members of the U.S. armed forces in Southeast Asia," said Senator Kennedy. He then told Fidèle Bastarache's story.

Congressman Peter Blute presented the Canadian Vietnam Veterans–Quebec group with a Certificate of Special Congressional Recognition on March 27, 1994 when they visited Massachusetts for Vietnam Veterans Day.

Later the same year, the Massachusetts House of Representatives passed a resolution honouring the Canadian Vietnam veterans and specifically mentioning Fidèle Bastarache. Massachusetts state representative Robert D. Hawke sponsored the resolution, which was seconded by the Speaker of the House, Charles

Flaherty. They presented it to two Canadian veterans on May 28, 1994. Hawke also presented it to Fidèle's mother, Helen Bastarache.

Charles J. Manca, the mayor of Gardner, Massachusetts, awarded a citation and a key to the city of Gardner to Canadian Vietnam veterans on May 30, 1994. Dorilla Bastarache is the keeper of the key, which has her brother's name on it.

A year later, Springfield (Massachusetts) mayor Robert T. Markel proclaimed April 2, 1995, as Canadian Vietnam Veterans Day. In part, he said: "I urge all our citizens to join with me in respect and gratitude for those Canadians who fought for freedom in Vietnam and in honouring the memory of our fallen warriors."

Bolduc also got recognition for two other Canadians. Gaetan Jean-Guy Beaudoin and Guy André Blanchette served in the New Hampshire National Guard, 3rd Battalion, 197th Artillery during the Vietnam War. On August 26, 1969, one week before they were to return home, an army vehicle struck a landmine and killed Beaudoin, Blanchette and three others. "I contacted U.S. senator Robert Smith of New Hampshire," says Bolduc. "He was excited to take note of the Canadian service."

Senator Smith read a resolution called "Tribute to Vietnam era servicemen from Canada" into the Congressional Record on Tuesday, September 13, 1994.

Bolduc sees his support for the Canadian Vietnam veterans as a traditional obligation, dating back to his grandparents' emigration from Canada. "My grandparents moved to the U.S. in the 1890s to work in factories," says Bolduc. "I feel like a Québécois expatriate."

Bolduc has also tried to ensure that other Americans and non-veteran volunteers are recognized for their assistance to the Canadian Vietnam veterans by nominating them for special awards.

He nominated Ric Gidner, Ed Johnson and Chris Reynolds for the Chapel of Four Chaplains Legion of Honour Award for their efforts in building the Vietnam Veterans Memorial in Windsor, Ontario.

The Chapel of Four Chaplains award commemorates four chaplains (a rabbi, a priest and two ministers) who gave up their own life jackets and went down with the crew when their ship was torpedoed off Greenland in 1943. More than 800 people who further the understanding and acceptance of the differences of others receive the award every year.

Bolduc also nominated Dominic Rotondo and Gilles Sauvé for awards from the American Police Hall of Fame on April 2, 1996, for their work in creating the Quebec memorial because it "honours the service of military police." They are the first Canadians ever decorated by the American Police Hall of Fame.

As Dorilla Bastarache carefully placed Bolduc's wreath at the Windsor memorial, she thought of all the things Bolduc had done for her brother, who had died when she was only fourteen.

At the dedication of the Windsor memorial, Vietnam veterans also left several items, including a steel pot (hard helmet) with camouflage cover; a boonie hat that still has red dust all over it from Jim, an American now living in London, Ontario; and a homemade wooden plaque with the Eagle crest from the 101st Airborne Infantry. That one has "from us all to us all" written on the back.

Mike Gillhooley was beside the memorial when a veteran dropped off his helmet. As Gillhooley went to hug the veteran, he bumped into his artificial limbs. "I had that helmet on," said the veteran, "when I lost my legs in Vietnam."

One of the veterans from Edmonton left George Tissingdon's military discharge papers along with a medical letter dated 1989 that advises that he could never work again due to a bad heart. Tissingdon died a few years ago.

Canadian military lifer Rick Pillage, who served in Vietnam in 1959, left a card and wreath at the Windsor memorial too. The inscription read "They that have shed their tears and blood with me, will forever my brothers and sisters be."

No one knows who left a heart-shaped wreath of red silk, a plastic wreath or all the additional religious artifacts: a wheat weaving and three bibles—one Gideon and two specifically designed for Vietnam veterans.

Other items have been left by Americans who wish to support their Canadian brothers. Americans have left T-shirts, an American flag folded military style, and a two-foot by five-foot plaque that says "Canadian Vietnam Veterans" and lists all the veterans' names.

The two monuments have affected local residents too. Beverley and Don Desjardins, the owners of Charlotte's Web florist shop, found out about the Canadian Vietnam Veterans Memorial in Windsor when several people ordered special wreaths made for the dedication ceremony. Since then, they often place fresh flowers there themselves. "We were putting flowers at the memorial on a regular basis, whenever we had a driver going to that end of town," says Desjardins. "There were a lot of vets who came on their own, who weren't part of the actual dedication, so we thought that we should keep fresh flowers there for the first ten days to two weeks, and then after that we just did it when a driver was in the area."

The Desjardins think building the Windsor memorial was a good idea. "Now the families of vets at least can come to a place where they can feel close to whomever is either missing or died," Desjardins says. "They have nowhere else to go."

CHAPTER THIRTEEN

From Need to Service

Canadian Vietnam veteran Ric Pillage is very happy these days. One of the veterans he's been helping for years just came into a windfall.

A Canadian who served two tours in Vietnam as a chief warrant officer on a helicopter and was shot down three times just got paid by the Veterans Administration. He collected monthly 100 percent disability cheques that had been sitting in the computer since 1972. The resulting payoff is hundreds of thousands of dollars—U.S. and tax-free. "When you get one of those," says Pillage, "you feel like a million bucks."

This Canadian might never have claimed his money if Pillage hadn't harped on it for so long. For the last ten years Pillage had been saying, "Go to the VA and make a claim." He was pleased that his friend finally took his advice.

The friendship between these two veterans and the positive result is typical of some of the life-changing results that begin to occur as veterans meet, find acceptance and then realize their own self-worth. For veterans, an improved self-worth leads to better mental health, which in turn often leads to even more community service. From angry people with medical and financial difficulties they turn into helpful servants who greatly benefit their communities.

Of course, it's not as straightforward as that. Most veterans follow a winding path towards a truly rewarding position in their community. Art Diabo, for instance, has been running the National Aboriginal Veterans Association (Quebec Chapter) since 1985. Diabo used to be quite active in the national Vietnam veterans movement, often attending veterans' conferences and helping other associations understand the Veterans Administration benefit system. "The common veteran doesn't realize that there's support for him," says Diabo. "He feels that he's isolated and going through his problems without realizing that a lot of people have been there before. That's why my experience helps them."

After assisting many veterans across Canada, Diabo began to understand himself. "During the latter part of the '80s and after the crisis, when I travelled a lot, I met with our brothers, I travelled to reunions," says Diabo. "That appeased me and answered a lot of the questions and doubts, especially within myself, about what happened in Vietnam." But he still didn't feel as though he belonged.

The crisis of 1990 refocussed Diabo's efforts on the needs of his reserve. The Kahnawake Reserve blocked the nearby Mercier Bridge in 1990 to support the Oka Natives who were fighting to save their burial grounds from being appropriated for the Town of Oka golf course. That's when the Canadian Army was called in to stop the blockade and take over the reserves.

The Mohawks dug in and ended up in a two-month siege. "It was almost like Vietnam all over again," says Diabo. "It did a number on a lot of vets. We were cut off from the world and we had to train people on how to defend themselves in the community—defensive-wise, on how to keep the outside forces from coming in."

As Diabo became a stronger and even more respected member in Kahnawake, he also began to accept a new role for himself and his community. "Prior to 1990, people were apathetic towards veterans' causes, you know," he says. "They didn't want to hear anything about Vietnam. But the crisis brought us all back together under a common woe, but we weren't off defending the United States or anybody else's agenda. We had to do it to protect our families."

Now Diabo's leaving the Canadian Vietnam veterans' movement up to others, while he concentrates on helping his people in Kahnawake.

As people like Diabo drop out of the national scene, newcomers with different goals take his place. Mike Gillhooley, for example, split away from the Toronto group a few years after joining to run the Canadian POW/MIA Information Centre.

Gillhooley distributes a newsletter about discrepancy and last-known-alive cases to a mailing list of about 300 people and on a World Wide Web page. Although he does get donations, he and his wife have been supporting the effort for the last two years. So far, Gillhooley has devoted all his free time and approximately $50,000 of his own money to distribute information about prisoners of war. "I wouldn't have become involved if I didn't believe there were live guys over there," says Gillhooley. "If people like us don't care about the accountability, then who will?" Eventually, he wants to help create an independent international board that will account for missing people after any conflict. "If there is an element of doubt in your mind," he says, "then just imagine what the families must feel."

While Diabo concentrates on helping Mohawks and Gillhooley helps the families of soldiers who went missing or were taken prisoner in Vietnam, other veterans work within the associations to create positive change. As the veterans' associations take advantage of previous success, they get better at helping their own members, and begin to look for others in the community who need support.

The associations have been particularly successful at upgrading dishonourable discharges for their Vietnam veteran members so that they can qualify for benefits. Many veterans who went AWOL (absent without leave) or deserted after their tours of duty in Vietnam ended up in Canada. That meant that associations here had to correct a lot of dishonourable discharges.

Monty Coles, who leads the Vietnam veterans' association in Calgary, helped veteran Mike Terry get his dishonourable discharge upgraded by writing several letters to the U.S. Army. Terry had disappeared for more than 200 days while serving in Vietnam. Then he just showed up one day in uniform to report for duty. This was a veteran who had already served in Korea and Vietnam. He had five Purple Hearts because he was wounded twice in Korea and three times in Vietnam, and he had already earned a Bronze Star. He was also one of the soldiers who got radiation sickness from bomb testing conducted by the army in the '50s. The veterans in Calgary knew that he didn't deserve a dishonourable discharge.

"We wrote letters to the U.S. Army explaining the situation that he was in at the time and giving reasons why it should be changed," says Coles. "It took about three years to change his status. In his case, they agreed that he was under a lot of stress from Vietnam."

All of the associations have helped at least one veteran turn a dishonourable discharge—something they refer to as "bad paper"—into a general discharge. This is just one way that the veterans start by helping each other, and that leads to active, supportive associations willing to welcome strangers.

British Columbia's Vietnam Veterans in Canada (VVIC) is the most active of these associations in Canada. What began as a small group of veterans led by Mark Klindt and Woody Carmack has become an active body working on behalf of up to 390 veterans.

VVIC holds the largest weekend event of any Vietnam veterans' group in Canada. Every year Firebase Canada summer festival brings hundreds of Vietnam veterans and their families for a weekend of camping, music, reflection and information on Stave Lake. Anybody who is affected by the Vietnam War can attend.

VVIC also puts out two publications, a monthly newsletter for active Vietnam veteran members plus a larger quarterly report for associate members, media and other interested people. They hold meetings twice a month, and active members always have someone to talk to.

VVIC supports all Canadians who served in Vietnam. And they're constantly finding more. Recently, when VVIC members found Al Geernaert, a Canadian who served in Vietnam with the Australian forces, living in a small town 600 kilometres north of Vancouver, they came up with a plan to show him he wasn't alone. "A bunch of us are going to Fort St. James," says Carmack. "We're going to have a barbecue and we're bringing some counsellors from the Vet Centre in Bellingham, Washington."

VVIC was the the first association to bring the Moving Wall, a smaller version of the Vietnam Veterans' Memorial in Washington, outside of the United States. They brought it to Vancouver's Sunset Beach Park in 1988.

Only two other groups of veterans, one from the Six Nations Reserve in Oshweken, near Brantford, Ontario, and another from Hamilton, have displayed the Moving Wall. Gary Befus, a Hamilton vet, spent hours searching for the families of all the Canadians he could find who died in Vietnam. He found the names of more than eighty families.

Newer associations take advantage of the older associations' networking and expertise. When they began the Toronto branch of the Canadian Vietnam Veterans Association, Mike Quinn and Mike Ruggiero used the American Legion mailing list to let lapsed members know about their plans. They also depended on the Veterans Administration office in Buffalo for assistance with getting disability pensions and medical assistance for veterans, especially those with PTSD. "It's really just knowing that you have a support group," says Ruggiero. "Knowing that there are other vets out there that you can count on."

Al Clause took advantage of the knowledge he had gained from the Toronto group when he and John Cogan founded the Canadian Vietnam Veterans–London association (CVVL) in 1993. Cogan and Clause registered the group as a non-profit organization three years later. Membership fluctuates around twenty to thirty people.

When they first started, Clause and Cogan concentrated on recruiting new members and they focussed on typical Vietnam veterans' issues such as Agent Orange, prisoners of war and PTSD. "Our biggest goal was to get somebody who could handle PTSD," says Clause. "We've got that now. We also have a service representative for Veterans Affairs in the States. The VVA sponsored him."

After that, the organization was set to take a different turn when Don Winrow became president. They began to expand their mandate to include family members more often. New associate columnists appeared in the newsletter, and family events, such as a Christmas party and a family picnic, were added to the schedule. Members still staff information booths throughout the year to try to recruit new members at public events in malls and at bike shows, but now family members also contribute to the association. They even participate on the board making priority decisions.

The newest veterans' organization was formed in 1995, after two Americans, Ed Johnson and Ric Gidner, donated a memorial to Canadian Vietnam veterans to the City of Windsor. They helped establish a new group of Canadian veterans, called the Memorial Association of Canadian Veterans, after the memorial dedication service in July. Gary Descaine, M.A.C.V.'s new president, has recruited eighteen members so far, seventeen of whom served in Vietnam and one veteran who served in Korea.

M.A.C.V. benefits from successful efforts by all the other associations in Canada. If they want to know how to upgrade bad paper, fill in disability claims or get help for one of their members, they have several associations they can call, although they frequently get help from the Veterans Administrators who work with the London association. If they want help locating a POW, they can call expert Mike Gillhooley. If they want to know how to attract members or run a summer festival for Vietnam veterans, they can talk to Woody Carmack in Vancouver or Lee Hitchins in Ottawa. Any association would be happy and eager to help.

They also benefit from the Royal Canadian Legion's extending of membership to Vietnam veterans. M.A.C.V. works with all six Legions in the Windsor area; they are all prepared to help by providing space for the veterans to meet or assisting to raise funds for veterans in financial or physical need.

Since M.A.C.V. benefits from the experience and efforts of all the people who previously fought for Vietnam veterans' rights in Canada, they can concentrate on new contributions to their community. Descaine's goals for his organization are completely different from those of associations created before. M.A.C.V. conducts occasional meetings and it wants to help veterans, but it also wants its members to be active volunteers in the community. "One of the members built a handicapped ramp for a little boy at no charge," says Descaine. "We're trying to do stuff like that."

EPILOGUE

The story of the Canadian Vietnam veterans remains incomplete. While some concentrate on raising a monument in Ottawa to honour their brothers who died in Nam, others help fellow veterans build productive lives for themselves. There are still those who struggle against mental and health problems that began overseas. Some of them have committed suicide, leaving family and friends struggling to honour their memories.

Most Canadian Vietnam veterans just live their lives as best they can. They either don't know or don't care about the movement for recognition and support, but they're the ones who will take over when others stop.

The individuals profiled in this book are thriving.

Robert Beattie is still married to his wife Elizabeth after twenty-five years. He is proud of his long-standing marriage and the wonderful son who came out of it. When he thinks of Vietnam these days, he wonders how the average farmer there is doing. He remembers seeing them in crisis and he is concerned about what their life is like now.

Al Clause still works for Ford, after twenty-five years. He and his wife Cheryl have been married for nineteen years now, and they have two sons. He just started coaching baseball again, which he hadn't done since before Vietnam. He's most proud of his work starting the Vietnam Veterans Association–London and their work helping veterans.

Art Diabo and his wife Marina will celebrate their twenty-fifth anniversary in March 1997. He is proud of their son, graduated from university in 1995 and is working for a family business on the reserve. Diabo spends all his spare time volunteering for elders and veterans in his community. He wants to make sure that they can live longer, happier lives.

Jacques Gendron just bought a new house and moved in with his girlfriend Louise. He is very proud of his three daughters. His eldest is a child psychologist and his two youngest are still in university. He is also proud of his success as mayor of Maplegrove, especially when he remembers raising funds from the federal and provincial governments to build an apartment complex for elder Canadians.

Mike Gillhooley spends all his spare time trying to bring prisoners of war home. "I've got the tenacity to keep going," he said. "It's important." He and his wife Julie celebrated their eighteenth anniversary in September 1996. He's proud of his son who finished university last year and recently moved to New York.

Richard Legault and his wife Nicole are still together after twenty-four years and they have two sons. Legault is proud of his international attitude towards the world in that he respects other cultures. As far as his time in Vietnam goes, he is happy to have been a credit to the French-Canadian reputation. He feels a brotherhood with the Americans he served with and with the Vietnamese people that they served together. He only hopes to meet his buddy Jerry Brasil again. Before leaving Vietnam, Brasil gave Legault a brand-new Seiko watch, saying, "One of these days, you're going to give that back." Thirty years later, Legault still has that watch.

Richard Malboeuf and his wife enjoy raising four children in Milton, Ontario. He spends all his spare time on board meetings for social committees and working with the Reform Party of Canada.

Claude Martin and his wife Michelle celebrated their twenty-fourth anniversary on July 1, 1996. They have two teenage daughters. Two years earlier, in 1994, he began dealing with his Vietnam past when he rejoined the Vietnam veterans' association in Quebec. Then he found out about the CAP Marines association and reconnected with his friend Ron Casto. After that, he visited the Wall in Washington in May 1996 to honour T.O. Green. And then, in the summer of 1996, Bob Bolduc arranged for him to receive his Vietnam medals, which he never got when he left California.

APPENDIX ONE

Canadians Killed in Vietnam

This list includes five men who were killed while serving with the International Commission for Supervision and Control (ICC) and the International Commission of Control and Supervison (ICCS).

John Austin Anderson
Rank: SP/4
Died on 5/13/68
Aged 21
Canadian Home: unknown
Home of Record: Williamsville, NY

Alfonso Paul Bartalotti
Rank: PFC
Died on 11/27/67
Aged 24
Canadian Home: Burlington or Hamilton, ON
Home of Record: Vallejo, CA

Fidèle Joseph Bastarache
Rank: CPL
Died on 5/27/68
Aged 22
Canadian Home: St. Antoine, NB
Home of Record: Gardner, MA

Gaetan Jean Guy Beaudoin
Rank: SGT
Died on 8/26/69
Aged 20
Canadian Home: Sherbrooke, QC
Home of Record: Manchester, NH

Alvin Kenneth Bencher
Rank: SGT
Died on 7/2/68
Aged 28
Canadian Home: unknown
Home of Record: Canada, XC

Vincent Bernard
Rank: LCPL
Died on 9/21/68
Aged 23
Canadian Home: unknown
Home of Record: Dorchester, MA

Guy André Blanchette
Rank: SGT
Died on 8/26/69
Aged 23
Canadian Home: St. Gerard, QC
Home of Record: Manchester, NH

Daniel Alphonse Bolduc
Rank: CPL
Died on 7/29/69
Aged 23
Canadian Home: Lennoxville, QC
Home of Record: Canada, XC

Gregory Lee Bomberry
Rank: SGT
Died on 9/6/68
Aged 21
Canadian Home: Six Nations Reserve,
Ohsweken, ON
Home of Record: Niagara Falls, NY

Ivan Clifford Broeffle
Rank: CPL
Died on 5/9/68
Aged 22
Canadian Home: unknown
Home of Record: Downers Grove, IL

Thomas Edward Brown
Rank: SSGT
Died on 12/2/69
Aged 23
Canadian Home: unknown
Home of Record: Canada, XC

Peter Norbert Bruyere
Rank: SP/4
Died on 5/25/70
Aged 19
Canadian Home: unknown
Home of Record: Canada, XC

Gary Butt
Rank: SSGT
Died on 4/3/71
Aged 19
Canadian Home: Chateauguay, QC
Home of Record: Canada, XC

J. S. Byrne
Rank: Sergeant in the Royal Canadian
Army Service Corps and member of the
ICC in Hanoi
Died on 10/18/65
Canadian Home: Aylmer, QC
Home of Record: not applicable

Michael Francis Campbell
Rank: PFC
Died on 4/26/68
Aged 26
Canadian Home: Cape Breton Island, NS
Home of Record: Canada, XC

Randall Kenneth Campbell
Rank: LCPL
Died on 4/25/65
Aged 20
Canadian Home: Pembroke, ON/
Montreal, QC
Home of Record: Canada, XC

Bernard John Caron
Rank: SSGT
Died on 2/9/68
Aged 31
Canadian Home: unknown
Home of Record: Canada, XC

Dale Stewart Chamberlain
Rank: SP/4
Died on 9/25/70
Aged 21
Canadian Home: unknown
Home of Record: Pasadena, CA

Larry Richard Collins
Rank: SP/4
Died on 5/1/69
Aged 22
Canadian Home: Winnipeg, MB
Home of Record: Canada, XC

Mark Paine Collins
Rank: SP/4
Died on 5/21/68
Aged 21
Canadian Home: unknown
Home of Record: Canada, XC

Andrew Charles Conrad Jr.
Rank: SP/5
Died on 8/9/67
Aged 35
Canadian Home: unknown
Home of Record: Millington, MI

Austin Morris Corbiere
Rank: LCPL
Died on 5/9/66
Aged 23
Canadian Home: Sucker Creek Reserve,
Manitoulin Island, ON
Home of Record: Canada, XC

Normand Alfred Corbin
Rank: LCPL
Died on 8/6/69
Aged 21
Canadian Home: unknown
Home of Record: Canada, XC

Frank Edward Crabbe
Rank: PFC
Died on 2/16/66
Aged 19
Canadian Home: unknown
Home of Record: Canada, XC

Donald Paul Davies
Rank: SP/5
Died on 6/29/69
Aged 20
Canadian Home: Lachine, QC
Home of Record: Canada, XC

Patrick John Dearborn
Rank: LCPL
Died on 11/2/67
Aged 18
Canadian Home: unknown
Home of Record: Canada, XC

Francis John Delmark
Rank: LCPL
Died on 8/18/65
Aged 22
Canadian Home: Lethbridge, AB
Home of Record: Salt Lake City, UT

Brian John Devaney
Rank: CWO
Died on 5/30/70
Aged 23
Canadian Home: Toronto, ON
Home of Record: Indianapolis, IN

Douglas Wayne Devoe
Rank: PFC
Died on 10/5/68
Aged 19
Canadian Home: unknown
Home of Record: Canada, XC

Richard Paul Dextraze
Rank: LCPL
Died on 4/23/69
Aged 21
Canadian Home: Montreal, QC
Home of Record: Canada, XC

Guy Douglas Dickie
Rank: PVT
Died on 2/8/68
Aged 19
Canadian Home: Hamilton, ON
Home of Record: Pittsburgh, PA

Michael John Dunn
Rank: SP/4
Died on 1/19/68
Aged 21
Canadian Home: unknown
Home of Record: Barker, NY

Gordon Patterson Eadie
Rank: LCPL
Died on 8/15/67
Aged 20
Canadian Home: Carp, ON
Home of Record: Detroit, MI

John Frederic Francis
Rank: LT
Died on 10/26/66
Aged 33
Canadian Home: unknown
Home of Record: Canada, XC

Thomas Edwin Fraser
Rank: PVT
Died on 4/4/70
Aged 18
Canadian Home: Six Nations Reserve,
Ohsweken, ON
Home of Record: Detroit, MI

Joseph O. Frigault
Rank: SSG
Died on 5/17/67
Aged 40
Canadian Home: unknown
Home of Record: Canada, XC

Gérard Louis Gauthier
Rank: A1C
Died on 9/4/67
Aged 21
Canadian Home: unknown
Home of Record: Canada, XC

Leslie Neil (Leo) General
Rank: CPL
Died on 5/1/68
Aged 21
Canadian Home: Six Nations Reserve,
Ohsweken, ON
Home of Record: Niagara Falls, NY

Danny Eric Goodwin
Rank: LCPL
Died on 8/24/67
Aged 20
Canadian Home: Nova Scotia
Home of Record: Brockton, MA

Larry Green
Rank: PFC
Died on 1/9/69
Aged 23
Canadian Home: Six Nations Reserve,
Ohsweken, ON
Home of Record: Niagara Falls, NY

Randolph Edward Hatton
Rank: PFC
Died on 11/14/68
Aged 28
Canadian Home: Toronto, ON
Home of Record: Canada, XC

Wayne Lindsay Hawes
Rank: SP/4
Died on 1/1/69
Aged 34
Canadian Home: Burnaby, BC
Home of Record: Canada, XC

Robert Wilson Holditch
Rank: CWO
Died on 7/2/69
Aged 36
Canadian Home: Port Robinson, ON
Home of Record: Canada, XC

Willis Francis House
Rank: MSGT
Died on 3/13/69
Aged 44
Canadian Home: unknown
Home of Record: Glen Burnie, MD

George Hudson

George Victor Jmaeff
Rank: CPL
Died on 3/1/69
Aged 23
Canadian Home: unknown
Home of Record: Canada, XC

Andrew John Jobey
Rank: PFC
Died on 4/29/68
Aged 18
Canadian Home: unknown
Home of Record: Canada, XC

Harry David Charles Kellar
Rank: PFC
Died on 2/25/69
Aged 19
Canadian Home: unknown
Home of Record: Canada, XC

John William Sidney Kelly
Rank: CPL
Died on 2/15/70
Aged 24
Canadian Home: Toronto, ON/Chester, NS
Home of Record: Detroit, MI

Bruce Thomas Kennedy
Rank: PFC
Died on 8/26/68
Aged 19
Canadian Home: Espanola, ON
Home of Record: Canada, XC

Robert W. Kenny
Rank: SGT
Died on 1/24/67
Aged 24
Canadian Home: Seely's Bay, ON
Home of Record: Canada, XC

Adolf J. Kroisenbacher
Rank: LCPL
Died on 3/7/69
Aged 30
Canadian Home: Austria/Montreal,
QC/Montmartre, SK
Home of Record: Canada, XC

Paul Stuart Laverock
Died on 5/1/69
Aged 20
Canadian Home: Toronto, ON
Home of Record: Perrysburg, OH

Charles-Eugène Laviolette
Rank: Captain in the Canadian Army
serving with the ICCS in Saigon.
Died on 4/7/73
Aged 42
Canadian Home: Quebec City, QC
Home of Record: not applicable

Darryl Dean Lawson
Rank: CPL
Died on 9/16/67
Aged 24
Canadian Home: unknown
Home of Record: Canada, XC

Kevin Douglas Low
Rank: TSGT
Died on 6/29/69
Aged 20
Canadian Home: unknown
Home of Record: Canada, XC

Geoffrey John Lukey
Rank: LCPL
Died on 10/6/69
Aged 20
Canadian Home: New Brunswick or
Nova Scotia
Home of Record: Canada, XC

Philip MacDonald
Died on 5/8/70
Aged 30
Canadian Home: Ottawa, ON
Served as a clerk with the ICC in Saigon.

John William MacGlashan
Rank: TSGT
Died on 8/3/67
Aged 38
Canadian Home: unknown
Home of Record: Canada, XC

David Karl Manning
Rank: LCPL
Died on 1/10/69
Aged 20
Canadian Home: unknown
Home of Record: Canada, XC

Maurice John Marier
Rank: SP/4
Died on 2/16/67
Aged 18
Canadian Home: Verdun, QC
Home of Record: Canada, XC

Joseph Henry Marshall III
Rank: 1LT
Died on 2/18/71
Aged 20
Canadian Home: London, ON
Home of Record: Almonte, MI

Alan C. Martin Jr.
Rank: SGT
Died on 3/8/69
Aged 22
Canadian Home: unknown
Home of Record: Canada, XC

Rob George McSorley
Rank: SP/4
Died on 4/8/70
Aged 19
Canadian Home: British Columbia
Home of Record: Canada, XC

Cyril Mitchell Jr.
Rank: SP/4
Died on 9/11/68
Aged 21
Canadian Home: unknown
Home of Record: Chelsea, MA

Regan Albert Monette
Rank: SP/4
Died on 3/6/72
Aged 22
Canadian Home: unknown
Home of Record: Canada, XC

Calvin Ian Nesbitt
Rank: PFC
Died on 4/26/68
Aged 19
Canadian Home: Guelph, ON
Home of Record: Buffalo, NY

James Paton Nicholson
Rank: PFC
Died on 5/2/68
Aged 20
Canadian Home: Charlottetown, PEI
Home of Record: Eliot, ME

Vernon J. Perkin
Rank: Corporal in Black Watch infantry
regiment of Canadian Army and
member of ICC in Hanoi
Died on 10/18/65
Aged 37
Canadian Home: Regina, SK
Home of Record: not applicable

Allan Wayne Persicke
Rank: SP/4
Died on 9/7/69
Aged 20
Canadian Home: unknown
Home of Record: Benton Harbor, MI

Ronald R. Philmore
Died on 5/20/75
Canadian Home: unknown

Roger Melvin Pisacreta
Rank: CWO
Died on 3/10/71
Aged 30
Canadian Home: unknown
Home of Record: Canada, XC

Gary W. Purcell
Rank: PFC
Died on 5/24/68
Aged 20
Canadian Home: unknown
Home of Record: Torrance, CA

William Reid Robson
Rank: LT
Died on 2/6/68
Aged 39
Canadian Home: unknown
Home of Record: Canada, XC

John Joseph Roden
Rank: SGT
Died on 10/11/69
Aged 26
Canadian Home: Halifax, NS
Home of Record: San Antonio, TX

Robert John Santoro
Rank: SP/4
Died on 8/14/68
Aged 22
Canadian Home: unknown
Home of Record: Canada, XC

Charlie F. Sauler
Rank: SP/4
Died on 10/4/67
Aged 28
Canadian Home: unknown
Home of Record: Canada, XC

Daniel Louis Paul Sauvé
Rank: PFC
Died on 4/21/66
Aged 18
Canadian Home: unknown
Home of Record: Canada, XC

Dennis Richard Schmidt
Rank: CPL
Died on 8/8/66
Aged 21
Canadian Home: Kentville/East
Chester, NS
Home of Record: North Plainfield, NJ

Stephen Joseph Scott
Rank: LCPL
Died on 7/14/68
Aged 18
Canadian Home: unknown
Home of Record: New Baltimore, MI

Larry Stephen Semeniuk
Rank: CPL
Died on 1/17/68
Aged 18
Canadian Home: Windsor, ON
Home of Record: Canada, XC

Edward Gerald Sharpe
Rank: PFC
Died on 4/25/67
Aged 18
Canadian Home: Pine Falls, MB
Home of Record: Canada, XC

John C. Sherin III
Rank: WO
Died on 10/2/68
Aged 27
Canadian Home: unknown
Home of Record: Canada, XC

Eldon Wayne Smith
Rank: SGT
Died on 10/6/68
Aged 21
Canadian Home: unknown
Home of Record: Waterville, ME

Frank J. Somers
Rank: SSGT
Died on 1/25/67
Aged 30
Canadian Home: unknown
Home of Record: Canada, XC

Tadeusz Sosniak
Rank: MSGT
Died on 8/30/68
Aged 27
Canadian Home: unknown
Home of Record: Canada, XC

Stefan Zbigniew Stalinski
Rank: PFC
Died on 7/8/65
Aged 20
Canadian Home: unknown
Home of Record: Canada, XC

Robert James Steel
Rank: PFC
Died on 10/4/66
Aged 19
Canadian Home: unknown
Home of Record: Canada, XC

Alan Macdonald Sturdy
Rank: SGT
Died on 7/2/67
Aged 22
Canadian Home: unknown
Home of Record: Redwood City, CA

Melvin Harold Suthons
Rank: PFC
Died on 6/18/65
Aged 21
Canadian Home: unknown
Home of Record: Canada, XC

Vernon J. Thorsteinson
Rank: CPL
Died on 8/12/67
Aged 22
Canadian Home: Winnipeg, MB/
Atikokan, ON
Home of Record: Buffalo, NY

John Douglas Turner
Permanent representative of Canadian
Commissioner to the ICC in Hanoi
Died on 10/18/65
Aged 30
Canadian Home: Montreal, QC
Home of Record: not applicable

Murray Dean Vidler
Rank: PFC
Died on 12/14/67
Aged 21
Canadian Home: Saskatchewan/
Vancouver, BC
Home of Record: Fargo, ND

Baxter Warren
Rank: SGT
Died on 3/27/70
Aged 21
Canadian Home: Cambridge, ON
Home of Record: Canada, XC

Rutherford J. Welsh
Rank: WO
Died on 7/27/66
Aged 24
Canadian Home: unknown
Home of Record: Canada, XC

Gordon Glenn White
Rank: LCPL
Died on 3/12/69
Aged 23
Canadian Home: Coaldale, AB
Home of Record: Canada, XC

Richard Claude Williams
Died on 1/4/70
Aged 23
Canadian Home: unknown
Home of Record: Langhorne, PA

Thomas Murray Williams
Rank: SGT
Died on 7/18/66
Aged 38
Canadian Home: unknown
Home of Record: Canada, XC

Paul Harvey Wolos
Rank: PFC
Died on 4/28/67
Aged 19
Canadian Home: unknown
Home of Record: Fargo, ND

Melvin Wright
Rank: LCPL
Died on 7/1/67
Aged 20
Canadian Home: Danville, QC
Home of Record: Knoxville, TN

Gerald Francis Young
Rank: LCPL
Died on 4/6/68
Aged 20
Canadian Home: unknown
Home of Record: Boston, MA

For an update of this document, please refer to the author's web page at: http://home.earthlink.net/~tarial/ If you have additional information, please e-mail it to: tarial@earthlink.net

APPENDIX TWO

Canadians Missing in Vietnam

Gilbert James Graham
Navy
Missing since 9/28/67
Aged 21 years
Canadian home: unknown
Home of record: Anaheim, CA

The navy first reported that Gilbert James Graham died in a ground battle on September 28, 1967. His status changed to missing on October 4, 1967, as his remains had not yet been found. The navy changed his status again in 1987 based on a refugee report of a sunken boat and dead American in the Hau Giang River. Official status: killed in action, remains unrecoverable.
(Reference #0843-0-02)

Johnathan Peter Kmetyk
Lance Corporal
Missing since 11/14/67
Aged 20 years
Canadian home: St. Catharines, ON
Home of record: Niagara Falls, NY

Johnathan Peter Kmetyk was assumed killed in a ground battle in Quang-Nam-Da Nang Province on November 14, 1967. The Marine Corps never recovered his body. Sightings of him were reported from Bangkok on September 13, 1991.
(Reference #0907-0-01)

Michael John Masterson
Air Force Lieutenant Colonel
Missing since 10/13/68
Aged 31 years
Canadian home: The Pas, MB
Home of record: Ephrata, WA

Michael John Masterson disappeared on October 13, 1968, when his aircraft got shot down somewhere in Xiangkhoang Province, Laos. His wife and daughter have been trying to find him ever since. In 1973, he was reported to be in Hoa Lo Prison, Hanoi. Seven years later, someone saw him alive, again in Hanoi. His likeness appeared in a Soviet documentary on October 2, 1991.
(Reference #1303-0-01)

Ian McIntosh
Army Warrant Officer
Missing since 11/24/70
Aged 25 years
Canadian home: unknown
Home of record: Canada, XC

The army reported Ian McIntosh missing on November 24, 1970, after his helicopter crashed in Quang Tri Province, about twenty miles southeast of Khe Sanh, near the Laos border. His body was never recovered.

William Marshall Price
1st Lieutenant
Missing since 10/12/72
Aged 27 years
Canadian home: unknown
Home of record: Kewanee, IL

The marines reported William Marshall Price missing after his aircraft crashed in the Dong Hoi, Ly Hoa, Bo Trach District of Quang Binh Province. They changed his status to killed in 1972, then back to missing in 1977.
(Reference #1973-0-02)

John Howard Reeves
Lance Corporal
Missing since 12/23/66
Aged 23 years
Canadian home: Winnipeg, MB
Home of record: Canada, XC

The Marine Corps reported John Howard Reeves killed on December 23, 1966, in a ground battle in the Quang-Nam-Da Nang Province. Although they couldn't find his body, he was presumed drowned. His gravesite wasn't found until eleven years later, though, in the Don Bong An Hamlet. His dog tags were found on October 21, 1992.
(Reference #0555-0-01)

Gary Francis Shaw
Army Private First Class
Missing since 11/11/67
Aged 19 years
Canadian home: unknown
Home of record: Toledo, OH

The army reported Gary Francis Shaw missing after a ground battle in Kon Tum Province on November 13, 1967. They confirmed his death on February 17, 1968. Then they received a photo from North Vietnam which resembled Private Shaw on December 25, 1969. Three months later they reconfirmed his death.
(Reference #0905-0-02)

For more information:
Documents pertaining to these cases can be ordered from the Library of Congress, Photodistribution Service, Washington, D.C. 20540.
Telephone 202/707-5640
Fax 202/707-1771

For an update of this document, please refer to the author's web page at:
http://home.earthlink.net/~tarial/
If you have additional information, please e-mail it to:
tarial@earthlink.net

APPENDIX THREE

Poetry about Canadian Vietnam Veterans

The following poem was written by Richard Malboeuf for the national memorial:

O' Canada, our home and native land
We had hoped you would understand
Why we left the safety of our land
To fight for freedom in Vietnam

Like our fathers before
We set off for a distant shore
Heeding the trumpets' call to fight
For a cause we believed was right

And though we served as Americans
In our hearts we fought as Canadians
Be proud, O' Canada, for we served well
In that time we spent in hell

And lest we forget those who gave their all
Their names are now engraved upon this wall
O' Canada, our home and native land
We hope that now you understand

The following poem was written by Ed Johnson for the Windsor memorial:

As long as we live
    You will live
As long as we live
    You will be remembered
As long as we live
    You will be loved
        M.A.C.V.
They Are Not Forgotten

The following poem was presented to the Vietnam Veterans in Canada by Laurence A. White, Jr. (Vietnam veteran, 1969-71), a member of the Vietnam Veterans of America, Chapter One-Eleven, Western Massachusetts, on July 9, 1994. It was one of the poems mentioned in his Chapel of Four Chaplains Legion of Honour Award nomination, which he subsequently received.

The Light of Liberty

Whose sons were these that left their
   lands
despite adversities,
Who wandered far and on their own
to face uncertainties?
For reasons known to them alone
they chose to sacrifice,
The lives they had and those they loved
for dreams and paid the price.

What was it in those dreams they saw
that others could not view,
While fires burning in their thoughts
compelled them what to do?
What words were whispered in their ears
that made their fears depart;
What spirit filled their minds and souls
put courage in their hearts?

The world was such a bitter place than
one that they had known;
They might have lived much richer lives
if they had stayed at home,
And yet they chose to take a course
where danger lurked ahead,
While loved ones pleaded not to go they
took that path instead.

What was the cause that drove them on
against their nation's will?
And why would young men take the
chance
of ever being killed,
If they did not believe the cause
that others questioned so,
Who criticized them as they went;
that they were wrong to go?

What men of greed would go to war
that offered little gains,
Or ever join a cause absorbed
with ridicule and shame?
No mercenary's heart could know
the spirit some men feel,
Nor ever fight for what "they did,"
preserving their ideals.

So many questions still to ask
with fewer answers found;
Why some men march to different beats
and hear a different sound.
Why some may see beyond the light
despite what they may dread,
and though they fear what they can see
they face what lies ahead.

They were your sons, O' CANADA
who saw that distant light,
And like so many thousands more
believed that they were right.
Perhaps not well remembered, though,
by those who did not care,
about the lives of men who fought
a war that wasn't theirs.

Their mothers and their families
remember them and know,
That they had been the sons they loved
who left them long ago.
No matter what was said or done
in casting doubt or shame,
Their blood was that of CANADA's
which flowed within their veins.

While those who fought along their
   sides
shared memories as well;
Of sacrifices each had made
while fighting in that Hell;
Of conflicts that were undeclared,
that offered no reward,
With young men of AMERICA
whose efforts were ignored.

What did they do that was so wrong
that they should be denied,
Whatever honors men can give
to others who have tried?
Perhaps the time has come at last
to think this matter through,
And understand why young men leave
to do what they must do.

O' CANADA; AMERICA
two nations closely bound,
Still guided by philosophies
where Freedom's voice resounds;
Who share a common destiny
that cannot separate,
Desires of a young man's heart
or PATRIOTIC fate.

No walls cast shadows that we see
to darken Freedom's light,
The torch of Liberty still burns
ensuring men their rights;
No armies stand in readiness
to threaten each with war,
Together we enjoy such peace
as few have shared before.

Though men may mock and ridicule
these feelings others hold,
Each man must trust the faith he has
in things that he was told;
And when he grows into a man
he cannot then divide,
Ideals he used to build his life
with honor and with pride.

If he believes in what was told;
what sacrifices mean,
He may someday have to defend
the right to keep his dreams.
Though others cannot understand
this sentimental pride;
Why some would rather leave their
    homes
than cast their dreams aside.

Like others through the centuries
whose lives were quickly lost,
They knew that Freedom had a price
and some would pay the cost.
So if those lessons they were taught
were lessons truly learned,
Then Honor is what they have bought
and Freedom has been earned.

Perhaps it is old fashioned
for PATRIOTS to give
their last and final drop of blood
So LIBERTY may live.
But it is not old fashioned,
no matter how it seems,
To face the dangers that we fear
may threaten Freedom's dreams.

O' CANADA, you raised them well
and they will always be
Upon a WALL in Washington,
which is their legacy.
But now within beloved lands,
These lands that they had known,
The spirits of your sons return
and now will rest at home.

In life they found no wealth or fame
no riches or reward,
No words of comfort for their fates
the living could afford.
There were no laurels to bestow
on those who did not win,
Except the laurels Freedom gave
Which they possessed within.

If men aren't meant to think or speak
with independent voice,
Then men should not have LIBERTY
that offers them a choice.
O' CANADA, remember that,
though men may disagree,
It is the truest test of all
that nations still are free.

The distant light that showed the way
and took them far from here,
Was one that casts its hopes upon
today and future years;
It could not be extinguished then,
though many men contrived,
And through the years the torch was
    passed
From those whose dreams survived.

While it may seem that men can choose
the lives that they will make,
It was decided long ago
which course these men would take.
For GOD would be the only one,
though some would disagree,
To light the path of those he chose
would face such destiny.

This Monument that you have built
must stand for them instead,
Not as a darkened place for tears
that shadows years ahead,
But rather be the light of hope
that all MANKIND may see,
For sons of CANADA became
the "Light of LIBERTY."

This poem was written by Ric Pillage

They that shed their blood and tears
    with me
Forever my brothers and sisters be.

APPENDIX FOUR

Vietnam Veteran Organizations in Canada

American Legion
Fort Pepperrell Post C.N. 9
P.O. Box 2316
St. John's, NF
A1B 4J9
709/745-1779
E-mail: jsayre@newcomm.net

American Legion
Department of New York
Canada County
Toronto Post 5
122 Bronte Rd., Apt. 1102B
Milton, ON
L9T 1Y9

American Legion
Ottawa Post #16 Canada
P.O. Box 59031
1559 Alta-vista Drive
Ottawa, ON
K1G 5T7

American Legion
Post 20
71 Bedwood Place N.E.
Calgary, AB
T3K 1L7
403/274-0543

American Legion
Charles A. Dunn Post 75
7044-141 Street
Surrey, BC
V3W 6L4
604/591-2185

Canadian POW/MIA Information Centre
41 Laurier Avenue
Milton, ON
L9T 4T1
905/875-0658

Canadian POW/MIA Information Centre–London/Canadian Vietnam Veterans Association–London
100 Main Street West
Otterville, ON
N0T 1R0
519/879-6205

Canadian POW/MIA Information Centre–Sudbury
407-119 Sandra Street
Garson, ON
P3L 1P4
705/693-1653

Canadian POW/MIA Information Centre–Toronto
Johnathan P. Kmetyk Chapter
190 Borrow Street
Thornhill, ON
L4J 2W8
905/738-0104

Canadian Vietnam Veterans Association–Calgary
c/o Royal Canadian Legion, Branch 275
755 40th Street S.E.
Calgary, AB
T2A 5G3
403/948-3219 (phone)
403/948-0654 (fax)

Canadian Vietnam Veterans
Association–Edmonton
14212-106 Avenue
Edmonton, AB
T5N 1B4
403/454-2710

Canadian Vietnam Veterans
Association–Halifax
P.O. Box 1608
Greenwood, NS
B0P 1N0
902/847-8778

Canadian Vietnam Veterans
Association–London
600 Classic Dr.
London, Ontario
N5W 5X8
519/453-1199

Canadian Vietnam Veterans
Association–Ottawa
P.O. Box 11375
Station H
Nepean, ON
K2H 7V1
613/284-0633 (phone)
613/283-9063 (fax)

Canadian Vietnam Veterans
Association–Quebec
250 Beausoleil
LaPrairie, QC
J5R 4Y8
514/444-4473 (phone)
514/686-1249 (fax)

Canadian Vietnam Veterans
Association–Quebec
5740 Coolbrook Avenue
Montreal, QC
H3X 2M1
514/739-6237 (phone & fax)

Canadian Vietnam Veterans–Toronto
P.O. Box 274, Station D
Etobicoke, ON
M9A 4X2
416/231-0872 (phone)
416/231-0513 (fax)

Memorial Association of Canadian
Vietnam Veterans
P.O. Box 25105
LaSalle, ON
N9J 2L3
519/322-4199 (phone)
519/326-3119 (fax)

National Aboriginal Veterans
Association
736 Granville Street
8th Floor
Vancouver, BC
V6Z 1G3
604/688-1821 (phone)
604/688-1821 (fax)

National Aboriginal Veterans
Association–Quebec
P.O. Box 737
Kahnawake, QC
J0L 1B0
514/632-7329 (phone)
514/632-5116 (fax)

Point Man International Ministries
5924 Oliver Road
Nanaimo, BC
V9P 6G6
604/751-2408

Point Man International Ministries
2880 Panorama Drive
Unit 112
Coquitlam, BC
V3E 2W4
604/944-0966 (phone)
604/944-7102 (fax)

Vietnam Veterans in Canada
25790-116 Avenue
Vancouver, BC
V2X 1Z6
604/462 0450 (phone & fax)
woody@vvic.org (e-mail)

Vietnam Veterans in Canada–
Okanagan Valley
S-10 C-7, R.R. #4
Vernon, BC
V1T 6L7
604/542-5238

Vietnam Veterans in Canada–
Vancouver Island
  #28-3230 Irma Street
  Victoria, BC
  V8Z 7B7
  604/723-5528 (phone)
  604/724-1232 (fax)

Vietnam Veterans of Yukon and N.W.T.
(lapsed)
  603 Cook Street
  Whitehorse, YT
  Y1A 2R5
  403/668-5821 (phone)

APPENDIX FIVE

Chronology of Significant Events

January 1945
Lester Pearson becomes Canada's first ambassador to the United States.

September 2, 1945
First Americans (First Lieutenant Emile R. Counasse, Sergeant Nardella, Sergeant Hejna and Corporal Paul) arrive in Saigon.

September 3, 1945
Chinese advance staff arrives in Hanoi.

September 6, 1945
First British and French troops arrive in Saigon.

September 13, 1945
Troops led by Major General Douglas D. Gracey (British), the commanding general of the Southeast Asia Command (Anglo-American Command which formally included Burma, Ceylon, Sumatra and Malaya; Indochina and Thailand were added informally) arrive in Saigon.

September 17, 1945
Vietnamese call a general strike in Saigon.

September 20, 1945
Gracey censors the Saigon press.

September 21, 1945
Gracey proclaims martial law in Cholon district of Saigon.

September 26, 1945
Colonel A. Peter Dewey, in charge of the "Embankment" project for the Southeast Asia Command (SEAC), dies in a terrorist raid in Saigon and becomes first American casualty in Vietnam.

October 1, 1945
Gracey's troops ordered to aid French troops.

October 9, 1945
British-French Civil Affairs Agreement signed in London. France gets full authority to administer Indochina south of the 16th parallel.

January 6, 1946
Ho Chi Minh (of the Viet Minh) is elected president of a provisional coalition Government of Vietnam.

August 3, 1946
Lester Pearson is appointed Canada's under-secretary of state for external affairs.

February 28, 1946
Franco-Sino Treaty pulls Chinese troops out of Vietnam the following year in exchange for French territorial rights to China.

March 6, 1946
France recognizes the Democratic Republic of North Vietnam (DRVN) as a

free state within the Indochina Federation of the French Union in exchange for re-entry of French troops to replace Chinese.

June 1, 1946
French announce formation of an independent state of Cochin China (which they had annexed in 1867).

November 20, 1946
Battles between the French and Vietnamese at Lang Son and Haiphong. French ships shell Haiphong. Six thousand civilians die.

December 10, 1946
Louis St. Laurent becomes Canada's secretary of state for external affairs in Mackenzie King's cabinet.

December 19, 1946
Indochina War (1946-54) begins.

September 1948
Lester Pearson becomes Canada's minister of external affairs.

November 15, 1948
Mackenzie King resigns as prime minister of Canada and is replaced by Louis St. Laurent.

June 13, 1949
Bao Dai arrives in Saigon to become head of state.

June 14, 1949
Cochin China government resigns to merge with Dai's Vietnam.

July 1, 1949
Bao Dai announces the establishment of the State of Vietnam. The Democratic Republic of Vietnam, under Ho Chi Minh, still exists.

January 9, 1950
Commonwealth Consultative Committee on South and Southeast Asia founded in Columbo, Ceylon. Committee included Australia, Britain, Canada, Ceylon, India, Pakistan and New Zealand. Australia proposes an aid plan to Southeast Asia which becomes known as the Colombo Plan.

January 18, 1950
China recognizes the Democratic Republic of Vietnam.

January 30, 1950
The U.S.S.R. officially recognizes the Democratic Republic of Vietnam.

February 4, 1950
The United States recognizes the Republic of Vietnam under Bao Dai.

February 16, 1950
France requests aid for Vietnam from the United States.

February 21, 1950
The Democratic Republic of Vietnam decrees general mobilization.

May 1, 1950
United States President Truman approves $10 million for Indochina, which goes to France.

May 1950
Commonwealth Consultative Committee on South and Southeast Asia meets in Sydney, Australia.

June 27, 1950
Truman sends a Military Assistance Advisory Group (MAAG) to Indochina.

August 2, 1950
U.S. MAAG (fifty-five Americans) arrive in Saigon.

September 1950
Commonwealth Consultative Committee on South and Southeast Asia releases a report called the Colombo Plan which promotes the economic improvement of a region which supplied food and raw materials to the world. The Colombo Plan provides training, technical resources and research to South and Southeast Asia.

December 23, 1950
Mutual Defence Assistance Agreement signed by the United States, France, Vietnam, Cambodia and Laos.

September 7, 1951
U.S. signs bilateral economic cooperation agreements with Vietnam, Laos and Cambodia.

November 1951
Senator John F. Kennedy visits Vietnam and announces that the people of Indochina do not support the French government.

July 1952
U.S. office in Saigon raised to embassy status. Vietnamese Embassy established in Washington.

December 30, 1952
Canada recognizes Vietnam, Cambodia and Laos as Associated States of Indochina within the French Union.

May 7, 1954
Viet Minh defeat French forces at Dien Bien Phu.

May 8, 1954
United States, France, United Kingdom and U.S.S.R. meet in Geneva to discuss Indochina.

July 7, 1954
Bao Dai, head of state for South Vietnam, appoints Ngo Dinh Diem as premier.

July 21, 1954
Geneva Convention partitions Vietnam along the 17th parallel, pending reunification elections to be held July 1956. Neither the United States nor South Vietnam sign the agreement. An International Control Commission (ICC)—Canada, Poland and India—is established to supervise the process. The agreement allows the ICC to establish fourteen fixed teams and as many mobile teams as necessary throughout Vietnam.

August 1954
Canada appoints Sherwood Lett to lead its International Control Commission delegation.

September 1954
South East Asia Treaty Organization (SEATO) formed.

October 9, 1954
French troops leave Hanoi.

October 24, 1954
U.S. President Eisenhower offers economic aid to South Vietnam.

February 12, 1955
U.S. begins training the South Vietnam armed forces.

April 1955
Canada appoints David Johnson to lead its International Control Commission delegation of 170 employees.

May 3, 1955
The International Control Commission releases its first and second reports.

May 18, 1955
The final deadline for citizens to move from North to South Vietnam and vice versa is reached. In the previous 360-day period, 894,547 people moved south and 5,940 moved north.

June 1955
The International Control Commission releases its third report.

October 23, 1955
National referendum in South Vietnam deposes Bao Dai.

October 26, 1955
Diem officially proclaims the establishment of the Republic of South Vietnam and becomes president.

Washington officially recognizes the Republic of South Vietnam.

December 1955
The International Control Commission's fourth report is released. The majority report, by India and Poland, lodges a complaint against Saigon for preventing citizens from moving north. The Canadian minority report outlines a plan by North Vietnam to prevent citizens from moving south.

December 12, 1955
U.S. closes Hanoi Embassy.

December 20, 1955
Canada recognizes the Republic of South Vietnam.

July 20, 1956
Geneva Convention elections not held.

1956
Canada appoints Bruce Williams to lead is International Control Commission delegation.

November 18-21, 1956
Paul Martin, Canadian minister of health and welfare, visits Saigon.

December 1956
More than fifty-one Vietnamese trained in Canada as part of the Colombo Plan.

January 3, 1957
The International Control Commission reports that neither North nor South Vietnam has followed the Geneva Convention requirements.

June 21, 1957
John Diefenbaker becomes prime minister of Canada.

October 22, 1957
U.S. installations in Saigon bombed.

February 1958
The ICC moves headquarters from Hanoi to Saigon.

March 31, 1958
End of fiscal year in which Canada gives $42,347 worth of aid to South Vietnam as part of the Colombo Plan.

June 7, 1958
The International Control Commission allows South Vietnam to replace war materials removed when France withdrew from Vietnam. Poland dissents.

March 31, 1959
End of fiscal year in which Canada gives $308,335 worth of aid (including $200,000 of food) to South Vietnam as part of the Colombo Plan.

April-July 1959
Terrorism against Diem government begins. Two American military advisers are killed in Bien Hoa.

December 20, 1960
National Front for the Liberation of South Vietnam (NLF, commonly known as Viet Cong) formed.

January 28, 1961
Within a month of taking office, U.S. President Kennedy approves a Counter-insurgency Plan for Vietnam.

January 29, 1961
Hanoi Radio welcomes the National Front for the Liberation of South Vietnam.

March 31, 1961
End of fiscal year in which Canada gives $172,606 worth of aid to South Vietnam as part of the Colombo Plan.

May 1961
Geneva Conference reconvened to discuss Laos.

June 1961
Geneva Conference agreement declares that Laos cannot sign alliances with, or accept military aid from, foreign powers. The United States will violate the agreement by the end of the year.

August 2, 1961
President Kennedy promises that the U.S. will do everything to save South Vietnam from Communism.

October 18, 1961
Ngo Dinh Diem declares state of emergency in South Vietnam.

December 11, 1961
First U.S. helicopter units arrive in Vietnam.

December 31, 1961
U.S. military strength in South Vietnam reaches 3,200.

February 6, 1962
United States sets up the Military Assistance Command, Vietnam (MACV).

February 18, 1962
Robert Kennedy visits Saigon and declares that U.S. troops will remain until Viet Cong are defeated.

April 1962
U.S. military strength in South Vietnam reaches 5,400.

Canadian delegation to the International Control Commission down to 100 people.

May 15, 1962
U.S. President Kennedy sends U.S. forces to Thailand because of deterioration in Laos.

May 23, 1962
Australia sends troops into Vietnam.

June 2, 1962
The ICC releases a special report which criticiszes North Vietnam for inciting violence in South Vietnam and supports a military agreement between the United States and South Vietnam.

August 1962
Canadian Commissioner Gordon E. Cox defends South Vietnam's use of defoliants.

December 31, 1962
U.S. military strength in South Vietnam reaches 11,300.

January 2-3, 1963
In the Battle of Ap Bac, 200 Viet Cong soldiers defeat 2,000 South Vietnamese (ARVN) troops. Three Americans die.

March 31, 1963
End of fiscal year in which Canada gives $308,335 worth of aid to South Vietnam as part of the Colombo Plan.

April 8, 1963
Lester B. Pearson becomes prime minister of Canada.

October 1963
U.S. troops in Vietnam total 16,500.

November 1, 1963
Diem assassinated in a military coup led by General Duong Van Minh, who respects the U.S. and agrees to continue fighting the Viet Cong.

November 7, 1963
U.S. recognizes provisional government of former vice-president Nguyen Ngoc Tho, new premier of Vietnam.

November 22, 1963
President Kennedy assassinated. President Johnson says that support to South Vietnam will continue.

December 31, 1963
U.S. military strength in South Vietnam reaches 16,300.

February 1964
South Vietnamese army raids North Vietnam and sends air strikes into Laos to prevent use of supply line.

May 2-3, 1964
U.S. aircraft transport ship *Card* sunk by terrorists while sitting in Saigon harbour. Terrorists also toss bombs at Americans inspecting the ship.

June 2, 1964
Canada appoints J. Blair Seaborn to lead its International Control Commission delegation.

June 18, 1964
J. Blair Seaborn visits North Vietnam Prime Minister Pham Van Dong. They discuss the likelihood of the United States bombing North Vietnam and the possibility of trade with the U.S. if South Vietnam could be stabilized.

July 6, 1964
Two Americans die in a five-hour battle at Nam Dong.

July 27, 1964
U.S. military strength in South Vietnam reaches 21,000.

July 30, 1964
South Vietnamese attack two North Vietnamese islands in the Gulf of Tonkin.

August 2, 1964
U.S.S. *Maddox* and U.S.S. *Turner Joy* report shots by North Vietnamese torpedo boats in the Tonkin Gulf incident.

August 7, 1964
U.S. Congress approves the Southeast Asia Resolution (now known as the Gulf of Tonkin Resolution).

August 13, 1964
J. Blair Seaborn visits North Vietnam Prime Minister Pham Van Dong. Pham Van Dong expresses anger that the U.S. should attack North Vietnam when the problems were contained in the South.

August 16, 1964
General Khanh takes over as chief of state for South Vietnam.

November 1964
Lyndon Baines Johnson elected as U.S. president.

December 1964
J. Blair Seaborn visits Hanoi and meets with Colonel Ha Van Lau, North Vietnam's ICC liaison officer.

December 21, 1964
General Khanh announces that the South Vietnamese forces will not support U.S. policy.

December 24, 1964
Viet Cong bomb a U.S. base in Saigon. Two Americans die, another fifty-two Americans and eighteen Vietnamese are wounded.

In Operation Barrel Roll, the U.S. Air Force starts bombing Laos.

January 2-7, 1965
In the Battle at Binh Gia, six Americans die.

February 7, 1965
Viet Cong attack helicopter base and barracks at Camp Halloway, near Pleiku. Eight Americans killed.

February 9, 1965
United States and ARVN army bomb North Vietnamese.

February 10, 1965
Viet Cong bomb the Qhi Nhon barracks, killing twenty-one Americans.

February 1965
Nguyen Van Thieu takes control of Armed Forces Council.

March 1965
J. Blair Seaborn visits Hanoi and meets with Colonel Ha Van Lau.

The U.S. Army, with the assistance of the Canadian Department of National Defence, tests nine different defoliant agents—Orange, Purple and Blue—at Canadian Forces Base Gagetown, Oromocto, New Brunswick.

March 2, 1965
Operation Rolling Thunder begins. Americans start bombing North Vietnam.

March 8, 1965
Britain releases an ICC report by India and Poland that requests that both North and South Vietnam reduce tension and aim for peace. Canada's minority report blames North Vietnam for increased aggression.

American ground war in Vietnam begins with the arrival of the 3rd Battalion, 9th Marines, 9th Marine Expeditionary Brigade, 3rd Division in Da Nang.

March 11, 1965
In Operation Market Time, the American navy blockades Vietnam's coast.

March 30, 1965
The U.S. Embassy in Saigon is bombed by Viet Cong. Twenty Americans die, another 175 are wounded.

March 31, 1965
End of a fiscal year in which Canada gives $557,000 to South Vietnam under the Colombo Plan.

May 1965
U.S. military strength in South Vietnam increased to 46,500.

June 1965
Canada's J. Blair Seaborn visits Hanoi and meets with Colonel Ha Van Lau.

June 12, 1965
Premier Dr. Phan Huy Quant resigns and Air Vice Marshal Nguyen Cao Ky becomes premier with General Thieu as head of state.

June 17, 1965
In Operation Arc Light, American B-52s start bombing Vietnam from Guam.

August 18-21, 1965
In Operation Starlite, U.S. Marines destroy a Viet Cong base near Van Tuong. Forty-five Americans die.

October 18, 1965
An ICC aircraft disappears on a flight from Vientiane, Laos, to Hanoi, North Vietnam. Thirteen people are killed including three Canadians—John Douglas Turner, permanent representative in Hanoi of the Canadian commissioner to the ICC; Vernon J. Perkin, a corporal with the Black Watch infantry regiment; and J.S. Byrne, a sergeant with the Royal Canadian Army Service Corps. The plane may have been shot down by the North Vietnamese, but no proof was ever found.

October 23–November 20, 1965
The Battle of the Ia Drang Valley, the first major battle between the American and North Vietnamese armies, lasts twenty-nine days. 305 Americans die.

December 24-25, 1965
U.S. and Viet Cong agree to a thirty-hour Christmas truce.

January 24–March 6, 1966
In Operation Masher/White Wing, the U.S. 1st Air Cavalry Division begins a search and destroy mission in Binh Dinh Province. 228 Americans die.

January 30, 1966
U.S. resumes bombing.

March 4-8, 1966
In Operation Utah, U.S. Marines fight the North Vietnamese Army near Quang Ngai. Ninety-eight Americans die.

March 7, 1966
Chester Ronning, a seventy-one-year-old Chinese Canadian who had served as a Canadian diplomat in Nanking during the 1949 revolution, as an ambassador to Norway and as a high commissioner to India visits Hanoi to meet with Prime Minister Pham Van Dong. They discuss an end to the U.S. bombing.

March 31, 1966
End of a fiscal year in which Canada gives $1,254,700 to South Vietnam under the Colombo Plan. Part of this aid was to build, equip and staff a tuberculosis clinic at Quang Ngai.

April 1966
In Operation Game Warden, the U.S. Navy begins operations in Vietnam's inland waterways.

May 24, 1966
Eight hundred men of the 5th Battalion of the Royal Australian Regiment land in Nui Dat.

April 1966
U.S. starts B-52 bombing in North Vietnam.

U.S. military strength in South Vietnam reaches 295,000.

May 26, 1966
United States Information Service (ISIS) library and cultural centre in Hué sacked and burned down.

May 31, 1966
U.S. Consulate and residence in Hué burned down.

June 14, 1966
Retired Canadian Chester Ronning makes a second visit to Hanoi to discuss an end to U.S. bombing with North Vietnam's foreign minister Nguyen Duy Trinh.

June 29, 1966
U.S. bombs the outskirts of Hanoi and Haiphong.

August 3, 1966–January 31, 1967
In Operation Prairie, the U.S. Marines try to clear areas below the Demilitarized Zone (DMZ) of enemy forces. The operation includes a key battle on Mutter's Ridge. 365 Americans die.

March 31, 1967
End of a fiscal year in which Canada gives $2,074,000 to South Vietnam under the Colombo Plan.

April 24–May 5, 1967
In the Battle of the Hills, U.S. Marines fight the North Vietnamese Army near Khe Sanh. 160 Americans die.

September 4-7, 1967
In the Battle of Que Son Valley, marines fight North Vietnamese Army. 114 Americans killed.

September 11–October 4, 1967
In the Siege of Con Thien, U.S. Marines hold the "Hill of Angels" from North Vietnamese Army troops wearing marine uniforms.

October 1967
Canadian Department of Health and Welfare and the Canadian Medical Association visit South Vietnam. The team recommends expanding the Quang Ngai clinic and creating a rehabilitation centre at Qui Nhon, plus others.

October 29–November 3, 1967
In the battle of Loc Ninh, the Viet Cong and 1,000 men of the U.S. 1st Infantry Division fight each other in the houses and streets of Loc Ninh.

November 3-22, 1967
In the battle of Dak To, the U.S. 173rd Airborne Division and the 4th Infantry Division beat 6,000 North Vietnamese Army soldiers. 285 Americans killed.

December 1967
Canadian cabinet approves $1.1 million rehabilitation centre in Qui Nhon (South Vietnam). The centre opens in 1969.

December 6-9, 1967
In the battle of Tam Quan, the 1st Cavalry Division battles enemy troops on the Bong Son Plains.

December 27, 1967
In the battle of Thontham Khe, forty-eight American marines die.

January 20–April 14, 1968
In the Battle of Khe Sanh, marines come under siege from the North Vietnamese Army for seventy-seven days. The final battle takes place on Hill 881 North. 205 Americans die.

January 29-31, 1968
Scheduled Tet truce cancelled. Viet Cong begin major attacks on South Vietnamese cities.

Viet Cong invade U.S. Embassy in Saigon.

President Thieu declares martial law.

South Vietnamese troops take over the roof of the Canadian tuberculosis hospital in Quang Ngai and Viet Cong toss a few grenades inside.

January 30–February 7, 1968
In the Battle of Saigon, 11,000 U.S. and South Vietnamese Army forces remove 1,000 Viet Cong from Saigon.

January 31, 1968
The highest daily casualty rate for the U.S. forces in Vietnam—246 Americans die.

January 31–March 2, 1968
In the Battle of Hué, the U.S. Marines face enemy forces in hand-to-hand combat throughout Vietnam's imperial city. 216 Americans die.

March 31, 1968
End of a fiscal year in which Canada gives $2,694,000 to South Vietnam under the Colombo Plan.

April 19, 1968
Pierre Elliot Trudeau becomes prime minister of Canada.

May 3, 1968
United States accepts Hanoi's offer to meet in Paris for preliminary peace talks.

May 5-15, 1968
In a mini-Tet offensive, the Communist forces shell 119 cities, towns and military installations.

May 10, 1968
Paris peace talks begin.

October 1968
Canada opens a rehabilitation centre in Qui Nhon (South Vietnam).

October 31, 1968
Operation Rolling Thunder ends. The U.S. Air Force lost 171 aircraft during the operation.

November 6, 1968
Richard M. Nixon elected as U.S. president.

January 13, 1969
The marines make the war's largest amphibious assault on the Batangan Peninsula.

January 25, 1969
Paris peace talks begin in earnest.

February 23–March 29, 1969
Communist forces launch a post-Tet offensive in South Vietnam. 1,140 Americans die.

March 1969
Nixon announces the "Vietnamization" of the war.

March 6, 1969
U.S. military strength in South Vietnam reaches 541,000.

March 18, 1969
In Operation Breakfast, the U.S. Air Force bombs Cambodia.

May 10-20, 1969
In the Battle of Hamburger Hill, 1,000 U.S. troops capture Ap Bia Mountain (Hill 937) in the A Shau Valley. Seventy Americans die.

June 1–July 2, 1969
During the Siege of Ben Het, a U.S. Special Forces (Green Berets) camp is cut off for a month.

June 8, 1969
South Vietnamese President Nguyen Van Thieu and U.S. President Nixon meet on Midway Island. Nixon announces that 25,000 U.S. troops will be withdrawn by thr end of August.

August 17-26, 1969
During the Battle in Que Son Valley, the American Division fights 1,000 North Vietnamese troops. Sixty Americans die.

September 3, 1969
Ho Chi Minh dies.

December 15, 1969
U.S. military strength in South Vietnam at 479,500.

March 31, 1970
End of a fiscal year in which Canada gives $2,970,000 to South Vietnam under the Colombo Plan.

April 13, 1970
U.S. military strength in South Vietnam at 429,000.

May 1–June 30, 1970
In the Cambodia Campaign, U.S. forces clear North Vietnamese from bases in the Fish Hook and Parrot's Beak and make the largest munitions capture of the war.

May 8, 1970
Philip MacDonald, a clerk in the Canadian ICC Saigon office, is found hanged with his hands tied behind his back.

June 24, 1970
U.S. Senate repeals Gulf of Tonkin Resolution.

July 1-23, 1970
In the Siege of Fire Base Ripcord, U.S. troops abandon their artillery base north of the A Shau Valley. Sixty-one Americans die.

November 21, 1970
A team of fifty Special Forces members makes a raid on Son Tay POW Camp near Hanoi to try to rescue fifty-five U.S. prisoners of war. The prisoners have already been moved to another camp, but the team kills the guards and advisers left behind.

December 1970
U.S. military strength in South Vietnam down to 339,200.

January 21, 1971
The hundredth meeting of the Paris peace talks.

March 22, 1971
U.S. troops abandon Fire Base Mary Ann after a one-hour battle with fifty North Vietnamese Army soldiers. Thirty-three Americans die.

March 31, 1971
End of a fiscal year in which Canada gives $1,970,000 to South Vietnam under the Colombo Plan.

Canadian delegation to the International Control Commission down to thirty-six people.

July 1, 1971
North Vietnam makes a secret peace proposal to Henry A. Kissinger.

October 3, 1971
President Thieu wins another four-year term in a one-candidate election.

December 1971
U.S. increases bombing of North Vietnam. U.S. military strength in South Vietnam at 160,000.

February 25, 1972
Hanoi and Viet Cong delegations walk out of Paris peace talks to protest U.S. bombing of North Vietnam.

March 23, 1972
U.S. breaks off Paris peace talks.

March 31, 1972
End of a fiscal year in which Canada gives $3,580,000 to South Vietnam under the Colombo Plan. Canada also hands over the Quang Ngai TB Control Centre to South Vietnam.

April 2, 1972
North Vietnamese cross the Demilitarized Zone (DMZ) with armour and artillery.

April 6-9, 1972
The U.S. Air Force flies 225 missions to hit North Vietnamese Army forces in and near the DMZ.

April 15, 1972
U.S. bombs near Hanoi and Haiphong.

April 25, 1972
U.S. announces it will continue Paris peace talks.

May 1, 1972
North Vietnamese take Quang Tri.

U.S. and South Vietnamese cancel Paris peace talks.

May 8, 1972
Nixon orders the mining of Haiphong and six other North Vietnamese ports and a blockade of supplies for North Vietnam.

May 10–October 1972
In Operation Linebacker I, 150 to 175 U.S. planes hit targets over Hanoi and Haiphong.

June 1972
U.S. ends its ground combat role in Vietnam. Less than 60,000 Americans remain.

July 13, 1972
Peace talks resume in Paris.

August 11, 1972
The last American ground unit (3rd Battalion, 21st Infantry) leaves Vietnam.

September 1972
Saigon expels the Indian delegation to the International Control Commission (ICC) after it establishes diplomatic relations with Hanoi. The ICC moves back to Hanoi.

September 15, 1972
South Vietnamese troops retain Quang Tri Citadel.

September 19, 1972
Hanoi releases three American POWs.

November 1972
U.S. President Nixon re-elected.

December 15, 1972
Paris peace talks fail. Nixon orders renewal of bombing to Hanoi-Haiphong area. The operation, called Linebacker II, begins three days later. U.S. aircraft drop 40,000 tons of bombs over the two cities. Forty-three Americans killed and another forty-one taken prisoner. Operation Linebacker II ends December 29.

January 8, 1973
Peace talks resume.

January 15, 1973
U.S. orders end of all offensive operations against North Vietnam.

January 27, 1973
Paris peace accords signed by U.S., the North Vietnamese government, the South Vietnamese government, and the Viet Cong. Joint military commissions institute a cease-fire, and an International Commission of Control and Supervision (Canada, Indonesia, Poland and Hungary) to supervise the peace process is created.

January 28, 1973
Cease-fire begins.

January 29, 1973
Michel Gauvin and 289 other Canadians arrive in Saigon as part of the International Commission of Control and Supervision.

February-March 1973
587 prisoners of war released by North Vietnam.

March 29, 1973
Last U.S. troops leave Vietnam. U.S. military role officially ends. A defence attaché office, a few marine guards, 8,500 U.S. civilians and fifty military personnel are left behind.

March 31, 1973
End of a fiscal year in which Canada gives $3,140,000 to South Vietnam under the Colombo Plan. The project includes creating a physiotherapy school in Saigon.

April 8, 1973
An ICCS helicopter is shot down on a flight between Quang Tri (South Vietnam) and Lao Bao (North Vietnam). Nine people die, including Canadian soldier Charles-Eugene Laviolette, an Indonesian officer, two Hungarians, two U.S. officers, a Filipino crew member and two North Vietnamese liaison officers. The helicopter had been flying fifteen miles off the safe corridor.

June 30, 1973
Viet Cong capture two Canadian captains accused of spying.

July 15, 1973
Viet Cong release two Canadian captains who had been accused of spying.

July 1973
The Canadian delegation to the ICCS leaves Vietnam.

July 1, 1973
The Australian Embassy Guard Platoon leaves Vietnam. (More than 59,000 Australians served in Vietnam between 1962 and 1973.)

January 1974
Cease-fire ends.

March 31, 1974
End of a fiscal year in which Canada gives $3,950,000 to South Vietnam.

August 9, 1974
Nixon resigns.

October 2, 1974
Canada announces a $1.7 million grant to the Canadian Save the Children Fund, the Canadian Council of Churches and the World Council of Churches for use in North Vietnam, including the rebuilding and re-equipping of the Hai Duong Hospital.

January 7, 1975
Viet Cong capture Phuoc Binh.

March, 1975
Canada announces an $18 million relief and rehabilitation program for Indochina.

March 31, 1975
End of a fiscal year in which Canada gives $3,000,000 to Vietnam.

April 20, 1975
Communists capture Xuan Loc. U.S. helicopters evacuate citizens from Saigon.

April 25, 1975
Canadian Armed Forces evacuate Canadians stationed at a new embassy in Saigon.

April 21, 1975
Thieu resigns. Tran Van Huong takes over South Vietnam.

April 27, 1975
South Vietnam assembly elects General Duong Van Minh to take the presidency.

April 30, 1975
President Minh surrenders unconditionally. U.S. military evacuates 1,000 Americans and 130,000 Vietnamese from South Vietnam.

Canada recognizes the Provisional Revolutionary Government of Vietnam.

July 2, 1976
Vietnam formally proclaims its unification as the Socialist Republic of Vietnam. Its capital is Hanoi.

BIBLIOGRAPHY

Primary Printed:

Government:

Canada: Debates of the House of Commons Official Report:
February 24, 1966; 1706-1707.
March 8, 1966; 2488.
March 15, 1966; 2708-2709.
April 26, 1966; 4302.

Canada: Debates of the Senate Official Report:
February 24, 1994; 173-175.
March 17, 1994; 213.
March 22, 1994; 250.
March 23, 1994; 267.
March 24, 1994.
April 19, 1994; 300-302.
April 26, 1994; 354.
May 10, 1994; 428-433.
May 11, 1994; 436-437.
May 25, 1994; 505-507.
May 31, 1994; 518-523.

U.S. Information Service. *Vietnam: The United States and Vietnam*, Volumes 1 & 2. Ottawa, 1966.

Secondary:

Books:

American Psychiatric Association. *Diagnostic and Statistical Manual of Mental Disorders*, 3rd ed., revised. Washington, 1987.

Bourne, Peter G. *Men, Stress and Vietnam*. 1970.

Cawthorne, Nigel. *The Bamboo Cage: The Full Story of American Servicemen Still Missing in Vietnam*. London, 1991.

Culhane, Claire. *Why is Canada in Vietnam?* Toronto, 1972.

Dean, Chuck. *Nam Vet: Making Peace with Your Past*. Portland, 1988.

Epp, Frank, ed. *I Would Like to Dodge the Draft-dodgers But...* Altona, MB, 1970.

Gaffen, Fred. *Cross Border Warriors: Canadians in American Forces, Americans in Canadian Forces*. Toronto, 1995.

———. *Unknown Warriors: Canadians in the Vietnam War*. Toronto, 1990.

Gwyn, Richard. *The 49th Paradox*. Toronto, 1985.

Jensen-Stevenson, Monika, and William Stevenson. *Kiss the Boys Goodbye: How the United States Betrayed its Own P.O.W.s in Vietnam*. Toronto, 1990.

Keylor, William R. *The Twentieth-Century World*. New York, 1984.

Moore, Harold G. and Joseph L. Galloway. *We Were Soldiers Once...and Young*. New York, 1992.

Patti, Archimedes L.A. *Why Viet Nam?* Berkeley, 1980.

Santoli, Albert. *Everything We Had*. New York, 1981.

Schneider, Jon (ed.). *Veteran's Album: A Photographic Memory Book of the Vietnam War*. Paducah, KY, 1993.

Stanton, Shelby L. *The Rise and Fall of an American Army*. Novato, CA, 1985.

Surrey, David S. *Choice of Conscience: Vietnam Era Military and Draft Resisters in Canada*. South Hadley, MA, 1982.

Taylor, Charles. *Snowjob: Canada, the United States and Vietnam*. Toronto, 1975.

Walker, Keith. *A Piece of My Heart: The Stories of Twenty Six American Women Who Served in Vietnam*. New York, 1985.

Articles:

Anderson, Alex. "The Forgotten Soldiers", *Maclean's*, November 8, 1993.

Anderson, James. "Canadian is Killed in Downed Copter", *Globe and Mail*, April 9, 1973.

Barker, Jeremy. "Vietnam's Forgotten Fallen Honoured at Last", *London Free Press*, July 1, 1995.

Benesh, Peter. "Plight of Canadians Who Fought for U.S. in Vietnam Muddled", *Toledo Blade*, October 12, 1986.

Bisol, Anna L.. "Canadian Memorial to List Gardner Man", *Montachusett Telegram & Gazette*, December 12, 1993.

Bridle, Paul. "Canada and the International Commissions in Indochina, 1954-72, in *Conflict and Stability in Southeast Asia*, edited by Mark W. Zacher and R. Stephen Milne. New York, 1974.

"B.C. Group Brings Viet Nam Vets Together", *Toronto Star*, May 31, 1986.

"Canadian Vietnam Vets Can't Get U.S. Benefits", *Montreal Gazette*, September 4, 1984.

"Canadians, Vietnam Role Remembered", *Winnipeg Free Press*, September 19, 1988.

"Ceremonies du Jour du Souvenir", *La Presse*, November 12, 1993.

"City Man Joins Fight For Veterans Honours", *Gardner News*, November 11, 1993.

Clark, Doug. "Canada's Unknown Soldiers", *Maclean's*, August 8, 1983.

———. "Our Forgotten Heroes of Viet Nam", *Toronto Star*, April 20, 1985.

———. "The Loneliness and Pain of Canadian Veterans of the Vietnam War", *Globe and Mail*, July 9, 1984.

Coren, Michael, "Canadians who Volunteered to Fight in Vietnam Derided and Ignored in their Own Country", *Globe and Mail*, August 10, 1994.

Danese, Roseann. "Vietnam Vets also Honoured", *Windsor Star*, November 13, 1995.

"Demonstrations Are Also Staged in Europe, Asia", *Montreal Star*, April 29, 1968.

"Des Canadiens au Vietnam", *le Journal de Montreal*, November 11, 1993.

Dona, Christina. "Vietnam Vets Refused Status", *Winnipeg Free Press*, October 18, 1987

Duckett, William. "Canadian Veterans Honoured", *Worcester Telegram & Gazette*, March 28, 1994.

Enman, Charles. "Ottawa Asked For Land For Memorial For Vietnam Vets", *Telegraph Journal*, June 29, 1994.

Farber, Michael. "Remembrance is Every Day", *Montreal Gazette*, November 11, 1987.

Ferguson, Paul. "Why Did I Fight Another Country's War? I Honestly Can't Remember", *Montreal Gazette*, August 7, 1988.

Ford, Catherine. "Canadians Should Honour Mercenary Warriors with a Memorial", *London Free Press*, May 5, 1995.

———. "Legacy of Terrible War Remembered", *London Free Press*, May 5, 1995.

Freidman, Matthew J. "Post-Traumatic Stress Disorder: An Overview", in *Encyclopedia of Psychology*, edited by R. Corsini. New York, 1994.

"Gardner Man Leads Campaign to Recognize Canada's Veterans", *Worcester Telegram & Gazette*, November 12, 1993.

Giedrys, Sally Anne. "Americans, Canadians Share Honours", *Gardner News*, March 28, 1994.

———. "Hawke to Sponsor House Resolution", *Gardner News*, November 11, 1993.

———. "Vietnam Veteran Honoured", *Gardner News*, December 21, 1993.

Gorham, Bob. "Vietnam Vets Share the Memories", *Halifax Chronicle Herald*, August 22, 1988.

Henderson, Gord. "You're Bringing Your Brothers Home", *Windsor Star*, June 26, 1995.

Hooper, Donna. "North Bay Man Works to Honour Vietnam Vets", *North Bay Nugget*, March 14, 1994.

Kennedy, Mark. "Our Forgotten Veterans", *Ottawa Citizen*, June 18, 1983.

Lajoie, Don. "Moral Code Guided Soldier", *Windsor Star*, June 26, 1995.

———. "Pain, Pride Undiminished by Years", *Windsor Star*, June 29, 1995.

Laughlin, Ann. "Vietnam Vets Forming Self-help Group", *Montreal Gazette*, October 17, 1983.

Laycock, John. "Vietnam Memorial Proposal Misguided", *Windsor Star*, May 4, 1995.

Leger, Dan. "Canadians Remember", *Halifax Mail-Star*, November 12, 1986.

Levant, Victor. "Quiet Complicity. Canadian Involvement in the Vietnam War", *Between the Lines*, Summer 1986.

Levy, Marc. "Americans Honour Canadians who Fought in Vietnam War", *Massachusetts Sentinel & Enterprise*, May 29, 1994.

Ly, Phuong. "Canadian Vietnam Vets Honoured", *Windsor Star*, July 2, 1995.

Mandel, Michele. "Soldiers Anonymous", *Toronto Sun*, September 21, 1986.

MacKeen, Cameron. "Canadian Vietnam Vets Battle Post-war Effects", *Halifax Chronicle Herald*, March 27, 1990.

MacLennan, Mary Jane. "Build your own cenotaph", *Winnipeg Sun*, October 20, 1987.

———. "Vietnam vets remember", *Winnipeg Sun*, November 12, 1987.

———. "Young Survivors of a Bewildering War", *Winnipeg Sun*, November 12, 1987.

MacQueen, Ken. "Canada Offers a Peaceful Home 20 Years After the Asian Conflict Ended", *London Free Press*, May 5, 1995.

"Metro Remembers", *Halifax Mail-Star*, November 12, 1986.

McAndrew, Brian. "Canada's Viet Vets Weep Openly at U.S. Memorial Wall", *Toronto Star*, September 21, 1986.

———. "Viet Nam Vets in Canada Still Feel Isolated", *Toronto Star*, July 6, 1986.

McKeague, Paul. "Canadian Vietnam Memorial Nixed", *Hamilton Spectator*, June 13, 1994.

———. "Our Vietnam Vets Shortchanged", *Windsor Star*, June 8, 1994.

McKenna, Brian. "Montreal March Orderly, Peaceful", *Montreal Star*, April 29, 1968.

———. "War and Steel: Brave Men Play the Deadly Game", *Montreal Star*, November 9, 1971.

Meersman, Nancy. "Loss of 5 Soldiers Remembered 25 Years Later", *Union Leader*, August 22, 1994.

O'Connor, John J. "City Joins in Honouring Canadian Vietnam Vets", *Worcester Telegram & Gazette*, December 24, 1993.

"Ottawa Demonstrators Find Embassy Closed", *Montreal Star*, April 29, 1968.

"Paint Defaces Cenotaph", *Winnipeg Free Press*, November 12, 1987.

Pemberton, Kim. "The Moving Wall", *Vancouver Sun*, May 31, 1988.

———. "War Memorial Seen as Likely Release For Troubled Canadian Vietnam Vets", *Vancouver Sun*, May 3, 1988.

Priddle, Alisa. "Canada's Role in War More Than Public Knows", *Windsor Star*, June 26, 1995.

———. "Coming Home", *Windsor Star*, July 3, 1995.

———. "Dad's Job Transfer Landed Son in Army", *Windsor Star*, June 26, 1995.

———. "Emotion Runs High for Vets, Memorial", *Windsor Star*, July 2, 1995.

———. "Flying the Canadian Flag in a Foreign Field", *Windsor Star*, June 26, 1995.

———. "If They Had a Law…", *Windsor Star*, June 29, 1995.

———. "Native Canadian Sought Glory in U.S. Marines", *Windsor Star*, June 26, 1995.

———. "Monument for Canadians Can't Find a Home", *Calgary Herald*, March 10, 1994.

———. "Shrine Brings Vets Full Circle,", *Windsor Star*, June 26, 1995.

———. "Vietnam Memorial Coming to City Park", *Windsor Star*, May 3, 1995.

———. "Vietnam Vets Close the Circle", *Windsor Star*, July 3, 1995.

"Protesters Active Around World", *Globe and Mail*, April 29, 1968.

Rabb, Jack. "Remembrance Day Approaching", *Smith Falls Record*, November 4, 1987.

"Remembering Sacrifices", *Massachusetts Sentinel & Enterprise*, March 27, 1994.

"Resolution Presented", *Gardner News*, May 31, 1994.

Rodgers, Paul. "No Plaques for 'Mercenaries'", *Western Report* (November 2, 1987).

"RCMP's Care is Canadian, Not U.S. Law", *Toronto Star*, January 2, 1969.

Seelye, Tracy F. "They Served with Honour, But with Little Recognition", *Massachusetts Sentinel & Enterprise*, May 28, 1994.

Semenak, Susan. "Memories of Vietnam Won't Go Away", *Montreal Gazette*, May 4, 1984.

"Senator Marshall Wants Site for Vietnam Memorial", *Western Star*, March 1, 1994.

Sheehan, Neil. "Pentagon Study Says Shakiness in Saigon Hampered Planning for Set-Up", *New York Times*, June 14, 1971.

———."'64 Air Strikes Deepened U.S. Committment and Reduced Choices, Survey Finds", *New York Times*, June 13, 1971.

Simpson, Anne. "Canada's Vietnam Vets Gather", *Washington Post*, September 24, 1986.

"Soldats au Vietnam", *le Journal de Montreal*, November 11, 1993.

Stevanovic, Gordana. "A Symbol of Unity for Veterans of Two Nations", *VFW Magazine*, January 1996.

Stretch, Robert H. "Psychosocial Readjustment of Canadian Vietnam Veterans", *Journal of Consulting and Clinical Psychology*, February 1991.

"The Negro in Vietnam" by Thomas A. Johnson, *Globe and Mail*, April 29, 1968.

"The Poppy in Vietnam", *Winnipeg Sun*, October 19, 1987.

"Thousands Take Part in American Cities", *Montreal Star*, April 29, 1968.

"3 Communists from Paris Talks to Speak in Toronto", *Globe and Mail*, May 12, 1970.

"Toronto Police Step in as Peace and War Groups Meet", *Globe and Mail*, April 29, 1968.

Treen, Joseph and Barry Kliff. "The Other Vietnam Veterans", *Newsweek*, September 10, 1984.

Turner, Randy and Ruth Teichroeb. "Vietnam Vets Gaining Respect", *Winnipeg Free Press*, May 26, 1991.

"Toronto Holds Nine Protesters", *Montreal Star*, April 29, 1968.

"20 Years Ago This Month GIs Closed the Curtain on Vietnam", *VFW Magazine*, Special Issue, March 1993.

"U.S. to Pay Health Bills for Canadian Vietnam Vets", *Montreal Gazette*, May 21, 1988.

Vander Doelen, Chris. "Candlelight Service Honours Canadians Killed in Action", *Windsor Star*, July 3, 1995.

Van Praagh, David. "Canada and Southeast Asia", in *Canada and the Third World*, edited by Peyton V. Lyon and Tareq Y. Ismael. Toronto, 1976.

"Veterans Groups Aim at Shortfalls", *Toledo Blade*, October 12, 1986.

Violette, Marc, "America's Forgotten Vietnam Vets: Canadians", *Plattsburgh Press-Republican*, December 6, 1987.

———. "Canadians Had Reasons to Volunteer for Nam", *Plattsburgh Press-Republican*, December 6, 1987.

———. "Tradition Ensures Respect for Mohawk Veterans", *Plattsburgh Press-Republican*, December 6, 1987.

Wageningen, Ellen van, "City Approves Vietnam Memorial", *Windsor Star*, May 9, 1995.

———. "Monument Stirs Up Emotions", *Windsor Star*, May 6, 1995.

Warren, Peter. "Legion Has No Monopoly on Remembrance", *Winnipeg Sun*, October 25, 1987.

"Was ICC Man's Death Murder?", *Ottawa Journal*, May 18, 1970.

Williamson, Linda. "Legion Closes Ranks", *Winnipeg Sun*, October 19, 1987.

Winrow, Donald. "Canadians who fought should hold heads high", *London Free Press*, May 15, 1995.

"Wives of 3 Canadians Lost in Vietnam Left with Little Hope", *Globe and Mail*, December 9, 1965.

Wormington, Joe. "Canadian Viet Vets Honoured,", *Toronto Sun*, July 3, 1995.

Wren, Christopher S. "Vietnam War Also Haunts Canadian Volunteers", *New York Times*, January 24, 1985.

INDEX

Chemin des Vétérans, 96
China, 36, 40, 147, 148
Cholon, 45-46, 147
Chretien, Prime Minister Jean, 105
Chu Lai, 40
CIA, 72
Clause, Al, 18, 31-32, 51-53, 61, 104, 109, 125, 127
Claymore mines, 50
Clinton, Bill (Governor of Arkansas), 72, 73
Clinton County Veterans' Service Agency, 83
Cochin China, 148
Cogan, John, 115, 125
Coles, Monty, 89, 123-24
Collenette, David, 105
Collins, Larry Richard, 131
Collins, Mark Paine, 131
Colombo Plan, 148, 150, 151, 153, 155, 156
Combat fatigue, 65
Combined Action Program (CAP) Marines, 41, 42
Comeau, Senator, 105
Commonwealth Consultative Committee on South and Southeast Asia, 148
Communism, 19, 36
Congo, 74
Congressional Veterans' Affairs committee, 82
Conrad, Andrew Charles Jr., 131
Corbiere, Austin Morris, 131
Corbin, Normand Alfred, 132
Counasse, Emile R., 147
Cox, Gordon E., 151
Crabbe, Frank Edward, 132
Cronkite, Walter, 20
Cuban blockade, 73-74
Czechoslovakia, 40

D

Da Nang, 40, 46, 48, 52, 87, 153
Davidson, Richard, 98
Davies, Donald P., 111, 132
Day, Gordon, 66
Dearborn, Patrick John, 132
Delmark, Francis John, 132
Demarais, René, 98
Demilitarized Zone (DMZ), 43, 49, 157

Democratic Republic of North Vietnam (DRVN), 147, 148
Department of Canadian Heritage, 105, 107
Department of Veterans Affairs (Canada), 86-87, 96
DEROS (date eligible to return from overseas), 60
Descaine, Gary, 126
Desjardins, Beverley, 119-20
Desjardins, Don, 119-20
Devaney, Brian John, 132
Devoe, Douglas Wayne, 132
Dewey, Colonel A. Peter, 147
Dextraze, Richard Paul, 132
Diabo, Arthur, 16-17, 27-29, 46-48, 57-58, 66, 67, 69, 76, 79, 84-5, 94-95
Diabo, Paul K., 17
Diamond Shamrock, 57
Diamond, Tony, 102
Dickie, Guy Douglas, 132
Diefenbaker, Prime Minister John, 132
Diem, Ngo Dinh, 150
Dien Bien Phu, 149
Dingwall, David, 108
Dioxin, 56
Disabled American Veterans Association, 76
Dong Ha, 52
Dong, Prime Minister Pham Van, 39, 152, 153
Dow Chemical, 57
Draft dodgers, 11, 58, 114
Duc, Thich Quang, 38
Dunn, Michael John, 132
Dupuis, Michel, 105, 107
Dupuis, Mayor René, 96

E

Eadie, Gordon Patterson, 132
East Germany, 40
Eisenhower, President Dwight David, 149
Erickson, Dr. Uwe, 67-68
Eskasone Band Council, 105
Evans, Charles, 83

F

Faires, Randy, 90, 95
Ferguson, Paul, 79

Tracey Arial is a Montreal-based freelance journalist who specializes in profiling ordinary Canadians who have unique experiences. Her work has appeared in the *Plattsburgh Press-Republic, Montreal Business Magazine, Montreal Gazette, Toronto Star, Kitchener-Waterloo Record,* and *The Financial Post.*

- Cap-Saint-Ignace
- Sainte-Marie (Beauce)
Québec, Canada
1996